TOP
Performance

TOP
Performance

HOW TO DEVELOP EXCELLENCE
IN YOURSELF AND OTHERS

ZIG ZIGLAR

WITH TOM ZIGLAR, HOWARD PARTRIDGE,
DAVID MATTSON, KRISH DHANAM, BRYAN FLANAGAN,
AND JIM SAVAGE

Revell
a division of Baker Publishing Group
Grand Rapids, Michigan

© 1986, 2003, 2019 by Ziglar Inc.

Published by Revell
a division of Baker Publishing Group
PO Box 6287, Grand Rapids, MI 49516-6287
www.revellbooks.com

Printed in the United States of America

Library of Congress Cataloging-in-Publication Control Number: 2019002502
ISBN 978-0-8007-3684-2

The author is represented by the literary agency of Literary Management Group, Inc.

19 20 21 22 23 24 25   7 6 5 4 3 2 1

Dedicated to P. C. Merrell,
*a Top Performer whose inspiration and leadership by example
had a lifetime impact on my performance.*

You can have everything in life you want
if you will just help enough
other people get what they want!

CONTENTS

Part 3 Motivating the Top Performer

FOREWORD

Top Performance is an incredible book, and it is more relevant today than when it was first published in 1986 and revised in 2003. I regularly use the concepts and teachings from the book in my keynote speeches and leadership training. Krish Dhanam and Bryan Flanagan, significant contributors to the 2003 revision, are still traveling the world sharing the wisdom of this book with corporate clients, academic institutions, and business leaders around the globe.

A lot has changed in the last sixteen years! Though these principles never change, the stage on which business is done is always changing. Because of this, I am very excited about the updates to this book and the way Ziglar Inc. has advanced to meet the needs of the business owners, leaders, and managers of today.

Ziglar has massive influence on social media with over 4.5 million fans on Facebook, www.facebook.com/ZigZiglar, and in the podcast world the *Ziglar Show* (found at www.ZiglarShow.com) has over 40 million downloads. Experts from every area of business and life regularly contribute because they know that successful innovation and change must be built on the foundation stones that never change.

I am very pleased to introduce two new partners of Ziglar and contributors to this revised edition, Howard Partridge and David Mattson.

Howard is the exclusive small business owner coach for Ziglar. We have been working with Howard since 2012, and together we have helped thousands of small business owners make more money and, most importantly, get their life back. If you are a small business owner, you will love Howard's chapter, "The Five *P*'s of a Top Performing Business."

David Mattson is the owner and CEO of Sandler Training, the world's largest sales training company with over 250 locations in more than 30 countries. I am so pleased that Sandler is the exclusive corporate training arm of Ziglar and is taking our corporate training offerings across the globe. David has worked directly with hundreds of CEOs to put together sales and leadership programs designed to help those companies grow and develop their key people. His chapter, "On Great Leadership," is packed full of insights you can use immediately.

Also included in this book is a chapter I wrote: "The Ziglar Performance Formula." I have personally presented and trained this concept for thousands of business owners and leaders with incredible results. What I love about it most is how simple and easy it is to understand and implement. When you share this with your team, they will "get it," and increased performance is sure to follow.

Developing excellence in yourself and others really is possible. In fact, when you choose Top Performance, you Choose to Win!

Tom Ziglar
CEO of Ziglar Inc.

PREFACE

Fifteen percent of the reason you get a job, keep that job, and move ahead in that job is determined by your technical skills and knowledge—regardless of your profession! That's what my late friend, human engineer Cavett Robert, said. What about the other 85 percent? Cavett quoted Stanford Research Institute, Harvard University, and the Carnegie Foundation (which, in the 1970s, spent one million dollars and five years on the research) as having proved that 85 percent of the reason you get a job, keep that job, and move ahead in that job has to do with your *people skills and people knowledge*!

I'm completely convinced he was right. As I travel around the country sharing ideas on personal growth, sales training, and the corporate concepts we teach at Ziglar Inc., I become more and more aware of the critical need for specialized instruction on how we can *manage* ourselves and lead others for maximum effectiveness. As I visit with professionals from all walks of life, I see common problems in many—if not all—of the different situations individuals are facing, and the common denominator in these problems is always the same: people.

So obviously, "managing people" (starting with yourself) becomes a high priority if we are to be successful. In this book, we have several primary goals relating to understanding people management skills:

1. We will identify the key factors in people management, including helping managers identify potential sources of conflict.

2. We will offer solutions to help overcome these potential sources of conflict.

3. We will share how you can apply the principles and ideas other managers have used successfully, thereby taking this book out of the realm of theory and making it applicable in the real world.

4. We will showcase practical Top Performance through real-life illustrations gathered from successful executives.

5. We will bridge the gap between training and development so as to create Top Performers who are truly performance champions.

John Naisbitt, author of *Megatrends*, says that retraining *managers*, not retraining workers, is the biggest challenge for the information-age corporation. With this in mind, the ultimate goal of *Top Performance* is to develop excellence in managers and to provide management with teaching procedures and inspiration to effectively develop and utilize team members.

The foundation for developing yourself and others is wrapped up in this principle:

> *You can have everything in life you want if you will just help enough other people get what they want!*

I have used this statement for nearly fifty years as a foundational truth, and never is the concept more accurate than when managing yourself and others. Important! I'm talking about a *principle* and not a *tactic*. As a tactic the words would be crass and ineffective. As a principle the concept works because it makes others *want* your leadership.

I read an interesting article in *Fortune* magazine about multibillionaire Li Ka-Shing from Hong Kong. He raised his two sons, Victor and Richard, in his business, requiring them to attend board meetings and conferences where they learned his philosophy.

Richard observed that his entrepreneurial genius father was involved in many joint ventures, most of which had great ideas and products but little capital. Richard's father taught him that if 10 percent is a fair percentage of the business you receive as a result of your investment but you know you can get 11 percent, it is wise to take only 9 percent. Li Ka-Shing taught his boys that if they took less than they could get, many undercapitalized people would bring their good ideas and products to them first. That's exactly what happened, because when individuals in the business world saw that these people were genuinely interested in them, they brought good deals to them, proving the philosophy completely. It's true! The great managers from all fields know that when they put people first, their effectiveness and efficiency improve.

One basic definition of *management* is getting things done through people. Successful managers recognize, develop, and use *all* their strengths by recognizing, developing, and utilizing the talents of their subordinates. They learn what makes people tick and transfer their own feelings of excitement and enthusiasm to those who follow their leadership.

Chances are good that if you are not already doing well in your chosen career, you are on the verge of a breakthrough to becoming more successful. Regardless of your chosen profession in life, *Top Performance* is written specifically for you!

INTRODUCTION

From the 2013 Edition

If you carefully read the title of this book, you will notice the subtitle is *How to Develop Excellence in Yourself and Others*. Obviously, it starts with you. If you expect to move up in the business world, you must start with personal efficiency and recognize that you will become a role model for others.

If you participated in organized team sports at some time in your life, you can probably recall the night before the "big game" and how the coach laid out the game plan. You went home with considerable excitement, exclaiming to your parents that the coach had really come up with something good and that your team was going to "kill them tomorrow!" Your faith in the plan enabled you to play the game with a great deal of excitement, enthusiasm, and confidence that you would win.

The game of life is considerably longer and a great deal more important; therefore, a plan is necessary for your expectations to be met. Your first concept or objective in the business world should be to attract favorable attention. Efficiency will accomplish that objective. However, the day will come when you need to realize that if you are going to be effective at management, there are certain things you should not be doing at all, much less doing well. Your objective is to replace yourself with somebody who may not have the experience and ability you have but who, with training and inspiration, you can bring into productivity at a more than acceptable rate. Your objective should be to produce other managers and leaders who can be more productive than you are. Some managers and leaders produce followers; you want to produce other managers and leaders.

Unfortunately, for too long there have been too many people who have believed that if they bring someone up to their level, all they do is lose a very valuable coworker who was making their department more effective. One classic example of the fallacy of this policy is that of Lou Holtz, the remarkable and outstanding football coach who built winners at North Carolina State, Arkansas, Minnesota, Notre Dame, and South Carolina. During his eleven years at Notre Dame, Lou produced ten head coaches. Obviously, his assistant coaches who became head coaches were his best coaches. So the question is, Where did that leave Lou?

The answer is quite simple. When word got out that he was developing leaders—that is, head coaches—assistant coaches around the country started applying to Notre Dame for a job as an assistant coach because they knew Lou would teach them how to be a head coach. Consequently, he replaced his good coaches with equally good coaches. He got a bonus when he acquired the new assistant coaches' high school contacts, but he also was able to maintain the high school contacts his former assistants had developed while they were with him. In short, not only did he replace his assistant coaches with equally effective coaches but he got a bonus in recruits as well.

You will quickly discover there is no sense of satisfaction or joy that equals that of bringing others along and developing them to the degree that they are as capable as you, so that they, too, can move into management. You can only be one you, but when you reproduce your abilities in others, your effectiveness multiplies and corporate America looks at you as someone to watch and promote to higher levels.

Bryan Flanagan and Krish Dhanam are men I'm proud to have coming alongside me, and their part in the revision of this book is proof of the joy I get from being associated with them. Let me share with you why I'm so excited to have their fresh and dynamic insights included in this revision.

Bryan and Krish come from different backgrounds, but their qualities and skills carry many similarities. Both have huge senses of humor, are strong in their faith, and are committed to their families and to being the best they can be in their chosen professions. Each is the personification of loyalty and gratitude for the privilege of teaching and inspiring others. Their messages of hope and direction are distinctly different, powerfully effective, and skillfully delivered.

Bryan Flanagan is a native of Baton Rouge, Louisiana, and a 1971 graduate of Louisiana State University with a bachelor of science degree. He began his fourteen-year career with IBM as a delivery boy while he was in college. While there, he served as a salesman, a "people manager," and a sales instructor at IBM's national training center.

Bryan worked with me for almost three decades and served as director of corporate training, where he designed and delivered customized training programs to increase individual and team productivity for companies such as UBS PaineWebber, Snap-on Tools, US Army Recruiting, American Heart Association, Salomon Smith Barney, Sterling Commerce, and many others.

Bryan and his wife, Cyndi, have two children and reside in Plano, Texas.

Krish Dhanam was born in the small coastal town of Vizag in southeastern India. At the age of eight he set his sights on America.

His educational background includes a master's in business administration and a diploma in international relations. He finished his postgraduate work at the Institute of Management Technology in Ghaziabad, India, and worked for a year in "outside sales" in India before migrating to the US.

After marrying his college sweetheart, he came to America with nine dollars in his pocket. He first worked in the United States as a commodities broker and then as a sales rep for two long-distance resellers in Dallas. He received a ticket to a Zig Ziglar seminar as the award for winning a sales contest. This initial exposure to the Ziglar philosophy led him to join the Ziglar organization in October of 1991, less than a month after he was sworn in as a United States citizen.

As the director of international operations for Ziglar Inc., Krish has conducted training in over thirty-five international venues and throughout the continental United States. His specialties are goal setting, change readiness, and service, but he also delivers programs on sales and communication.

An active participant in the Indian community of Dallas, Krish sits on the board of directors for the Greater Dallas Indo-American Chamber of Commerce and is also an advisory director to Ipelion, an e-business consulting and IT services firm.

Krish, his wife, Anila, and their son, Nicolas, make their home in Flower Mound, Texas.

I'm excited to share the pages of this book with Bryan and Krish because for many years they have applied the practical tools and motivational principles I have written about in this book. They truly exemplify the principles *Top Performance* teaches.

Now let's get into the body of this book and see what's important in building and developing a permanent career.

PART 1

THE ART OF
TOP
Performance

The object of art is to crystallize emotion
into thoughts and then fix it in form.

Delsarte

1

Building a Foundation

No legitimate business man ever got started on the road to permanent success by any other means than that of hard, intelligent work, coupled with an earned credit, plus character.

Timothy Dwight

A good architect/engineer, knowing the purpose for a specific building, can tell you how high it will be based on the depth of the hole in the ground. In short, the foundation is what he or she will build on. In life, our foundation stones are the things that will determine to a very large degree how high we will climb and, more importantly, how long we will maintain those lofty positions. Integrity, which means "basic wholeness," is essential to that foundation.

It's true that a pleasing personality helps win friends and influence people. However, when we add character and integrity to that formula, we are able to keep those friends and maintain the influence.

In a 2002 study in *Psychological Reports* entitled "Goal-Directedness and Personal Identity as Correlates of Life Outcomes," Dr. Barry M. Goldman, Dr. Edwin A. Locke, and David G. Jensen found that your values, motives, confidence, and philosophy of life have a direct bearing on your self-image, and in 1985 Dr. S. Kahn and colleagues found that self-image is associated with life happiness and satisfaction, personal well-being, and marital satisfaction. It's true. Our values impact every aspect of our lives. It would be difficult to imagine that a person who was a liar and a thief could have a healthy self-image. Needless to say, he or she would not expect to have a long-term, happy business or personal life.

Laurel Cutler, past vice chairman of FCB Leber Katz Partners, said, "Values determine behavior, behavior determines reputation, reputation determines advantages." From a personal perspective, a number of years ago I was in the market for a new Cadillac. I shopped at two dealerships, decided exactly which color and model I wanted, and was talking about it with a friend. He suggested I not do anything until I talked to Chuck Bellows at Rodger Meier Cadillac. He assured me that what Chuck told me I could absolutely depend on—his integrity was complete.

I went to see Chuck Bellows, and twenty minutes later we had made a deal for the automobile. The reason I decided so quickly was that Chuck had been working on me for twenty-three years. I realize that sounds like a contradiction, but twenty-three years earlier he had made the decision that he would spend his career selling Cadillacs at Rodger Meier Cadillac. To do that he knew he had to build a reputation on integrity. He had done that. When I went to see Chuck Bellows, I did not go to look at a Cadillac; I'd already done that. I went to *buy* a Cadillac. Yes, reputation—if it's a good one—has serious advantages.

It's a matter of fact that *The New England Primer*, based on Puritan values and readings from the Bible, was taught for nearly two hundred years in our public educational system and that of the first 108 schools and universities founded in America, 106 were founded to teach Christian values. The biblical principles that were taught then are actually ridiculed today, along with the people who claim Christian values and profess Christianity. I challenge you to explore character very deeply as you build your career. There is a reason the leaders of yesterday had more integrity than the leaders of today.

We will also deal with trust in our relationships as we go along, but for now I will simply state that all long-term, happy, successful relationships are built on trust, and trust definitely affects national performance. Francis Fukuyama wrote the book *Trust: The Social Virtues and the Creation of Prosperity*. He studied several cultures over several generations and concluded that the progress of a nation could be measured by the level of trust in that nation.

There is a huge lack of trust in our society today, and that lack of trust has impacted our economy. Corporate scandals have resulted in the loss of untold billions of dollars. Tens of thousands of retirement funds have been depleted, thousands of jobs have been eliminated, and confidence in life itself has been damaged for millions of people. As a nation, we have come to realize that we must look toward reinstating our character qualities in every phase of our lives. As you move up in the corporate world, your success will be largely measured by the amount of trust others have in you combined with your effectiveness in what you do.

Just how important is trust? One study reported by Walker Information and Hudson Institute revealed that if the associates and employees did not think management was ethical, only 9 percent of them were committed to staying where they were. On the other hand, if trust in management was evident, 55 percent of them had every intention of staying where they were. Since the cost of replacing valued employees is enormous, creating a foundation of trust is essential to having a successful business.

In the world of sales, we have long known that of the five major reasons people do not buy—no need, no money, no hurry, no desire, no trust— the last one is the biggie. Most prospects will not arbitrarily say, "You know you're stretching the truth," or "You're lying about this," but there is something they just *feel*. Because they *feel* that something is amiss, they simply do not buy.

While the main thrust of *Top Performance* will be in the management and personal responsibility area, we will also recognize the fact that in small companies the leader and the manager are often the same person. The example I use of my mother with her family (which you'll read about in chapter 4) clearly shows how managers are often leaders as well.

Creativity has a critical role in the leadership/management world— not only creativity on your part, but your ability to teach your people by example how to be creative. It's important that you understand that the more you know about any one subject, the more creative you will become as you expand your knowledge in any area.

A classic example is my book *Secrets of Closing the Sale*. I wrote the book after I had been in the selling profession for thirty-six years. As a result, I was knowledgeable about the profession. Several years before I wrote the book, I had read an article that included three short paragraphs entitled "The Heart of the Sale." I took those three short paragraphs, which included several gems that triggered new approaches to the information I had already acquired through experience, and expanded them into seventy pages of my book. New information triggers the imagination, and creative ideas result.

One of the classic examples of creativity under even the most unusual circumstances is this simple little example: Matt Boswell is in the dog-waste removal business, and his promotion is truly unique. On his business card it states, "Too Pooped to Scoop? Reclaim your yard. The Pet Butler. Picking up where your dog left off since 1998." Then, "Our business stinks but it's picking up." His name, "Matt Boswell, Entre-manure." He's actually a "Fecal Matter Removal Technician" and claims to be "Number One in the Number Two Business." He closes out his card, "For Dogs on the Go" and "Not Too Cool to Get the Stool. Your Pet's Business Is Our Business."

Chances are good you won't go into competition with Matt Boswell, but it is safe to say that he used his creativity effectively to build a business—and you can use yours to improve your business. Integrity, character/values, trust, and creativity make up the cornerstones of your foundation for management style, leadership style, and lifestyle.

PERFORMANCE PRINCIPLES

1. Your foundation determines how successful you will be.
2. Integrity, character/values, trust, and creativity are the four cornerstones of a good foundation.
3. Creativity pulls everything together.

2

Choosing to Be a Top Performer

We are free up to the point of choice, then the choice controls the chooser.

Mary Crowley

Our success in life is determined by the choices we make. You are going to be making choices that will determine your success as you learn to manage yourself and others. To be effective in making proper choices, you must understand the difference between *reacting* and *responding*.

One January I was in Kansas City, Missouri. It had been one of those weeks. As we'd say down home, "I've been drove hard and hung up wet!" I wasn't just whipped—I was *whupped*! And there is a difference. That particular morning I had a lengthy recording session. When I record, of necessity I must turn up my volume and tempo a couple of notches. The only means of communication I have on a recording is my voice, so I must utilize it to the fullest or the people who listen to the recording might let their minds drift and miss the message.

That morning for four solid hours the session was wide open, full speed ahead, no holds barred. (I speak at about 280 words a minute with gusts up to 450.) I finished at exactly 1:00 p.m., and since we had a 3:00 p.m. departure time for Dallas, we had to hurry. The airline had told us to get to the airport at least an hour early to secure our recording equipment, which is very heavy and bulky. My son-in-law, Chad Witmeyer, who was the general manager for At the Top, the recording and cassette-duplication corporation we ran at the time, packed our gear as quickly as possible, and the two of us made a mad dash for the airport, which was a thirty-minute trip from downtown Kansas City.

We pulled into the airport at exactly 2:00 p.m. There were two long lines, and we selected the shorter of the two. I noticed almost immediately that one of the ticket agents was walking around behind the counter, and I saw a Position Closed sign at one end. My experience told me she would remove Position Closed and replace it with Position Open, so I mentally and physically got ready to make a quick dash to the counter when she opened the other line. In a matter of minutes she walked over to the Position Closed sign, flipped it to Position Open, and smilingly announced to the group, "Those of you who have a seat on the three o'clock flight to Dallas come over here."

Surprise, Surprise!

Quick as a flash, I ran to her position and was first in line. The ticket agent looked at me, smiled, and said, "The three o'clock flight to Dallas has been canceled." To this I enthusiastically responded, "Fantastic!" When I said that, the ticket agent, with a puzzled expression on her face, asked, "Now, why in the world would you say, 'Fantastic,' when I've just told you the three o'clock flight to Dallas has been canceled?" I smiled back at her and said, "Ma'am, there are only three reasons why anybody would cancel a flight to Dallas, Texas. Number one, something must be wrong with that airplane; number two, something must be wrong with the person who is going to fly that airplane; number three, something must be wrong with the weather they're going to fly that airplane in. Now, ma'am, if any one of those three situations exists, I don't want to be up there. I want to be right down here! Fantastic!"

Hot Dog, I've Got Some Bad News for You!

Have you ever noticed how some people seem to delight in delivering bad news? It's as if they just can't wait to let you know that life is tough and you're in for a tough time. To my response, the ticket agent put her hands on her hips in an authoritative, "I'm not through with you yet" kind of position and said, "Yes, but the next flight doesn't leave until 6:05." To that I responded, "Fantastic!"

By now the other two lines of people were looking in my direction and undoubtedly wondering, *Who is that nut who says everything is fantastic?* The ticket agent herself looked at me in complete shock and said, "Now I'm really puzzled. Why in the world would you say, 'Fantastic,' when I've just told you that you've got a four-hour wait in the airport in Kansas City, Missouri?" "Why," I said, "ma'am, it's really very simple. In all my years of living, never before in my entire life have I had a chance to spend four hours in the Kansas City, Missouri, airport. Do you realize that at this moment there are literally tens of millions of people on the face of this earth who not only are cold but also are hungry? Here I am in a beautiful facility, and even though it's cold outside, it's comfortable inside. Down the corridor is a nice little coffee shop. I'm going to go down there, relax for a few minutes, and enjoy a cup of coffee. Then I've got some extremely important work that I need to do, and here I am in one of the nicest buildings in the whole area. It is easily the biggest, most comfortable, rent-free office I've ever had at my disposal. Fantastic!"

That's Pretty Strong—Even for Positive Thinkers

Now, I'm reasonably confident you may be saying to yourself, "Ziglar, I'll go along with a lot of this 'positive thinking' stuff, but man, that's a little strong!" You may even be saying to yourself, "I wonder if he *really* did say that?" As we'd say down home, "On my scout's honor, that's exactly what I said."

To this you may well say, "Okay, Ziglar, you said it. But now tell me the truth—did you really *feel* that way?" To this I respond, "Of course not!" At least initially I didn't really feel that way. Like most travelers who've had a tough week on the road, I would have preferred to have been on my way home, but for the next four hours I did not have that option. However, I did have two other options to choose from. I could have chosen to *respond*—which is positive—or I could have chosen to *react*—which is negative. I chose to respond.

If *react* and *respond* sound like the same thing to you, let me explain the difference. You go to the doctor, who gives you a prescription and tells you to come back the next day. When you go back, if he looks worried and tells you he needs to change the prescription because your body is *reacting* to the medicine, you're probably going to be concerned. On the other hand, if he tells you your body is *responding* to the medicine, you're going to smile because you know you're on your way to recovery. So, to react is negative and to respond is positive—the choice is yours! It's a fact that *you can't tailor-make the situations in life, but you can tailor-make the attitudes to fit those situations before they arise.*

When the ticket agent told me my flight had been canceled, I could have reacted sarcastically and said, "That's great! That's just great! I've had reservations for this flight for over a month, and I've done everything you've told me to do, including nearly breaking my neck to get here an hour early. All I need is my boarding pass and my seat assignment, but without explanation and without apology you tell me somebody has canceled my flight! Well, I want to know why the flight was canceled! As I drove up I saw several of your airplanes sitting out on the runway, not doing a thing. Why can't you take one of them and fly us to Dallas like you are supposed to? What are they doing out there anyhow? Who made the bright decision to cancel my flight to Dallas, Texas?" I could have reacted in that sarcastic manner. *And the next flight still leaves at 6:05!*

(Many years after this incident, Krish Dhanam repeated a version of this behavior in another airport and was asked, "What are you? Some kind of Zig Ziglar?")

Respond—for a Better Tomorrow

Now, my reading friend, there are some things you simply are not going to change. I don't care how much thought you give it, you're not going to add a single cubit to your height. You're not going to change when you were born, where you were born, how you were born, or to whom you were born. As a matter of fact, you're not going to change one single whisper that's taken place in the *yesterdays* of your life.

Tomorrow is a different subject. Regardless of your past, your tomorrow is a clean slate. You can choose what you want to write on that slate. You make that choice each time you decide to *respond* or *react* to negative events. As a manager, when your employees act in a rude, thoughtless, and inconsiderate manner and are impossible to deal with, please understand you can still *choose* to respond or react. Your choice will play a major role in your relationship with your employees. Obviously this doesn't mean that to lead others you, the manager, must be "perfect" and never blow your cool. Not only is that unrealistic, it is impossible—and maybe even undesirable. After all, managers are people too, and our employees need to know we are human and have feelings. On balance, however, we need to be careful that we choose to respond far more often than we choose to react, and that when we react, it is under control and directed to the *action* the person took and not to the employee personally.

My friend Fred Smith, now deceased, was truly one of the outstanding consultants and management experts in America. He gave helpful advice on this matter in his excellent book *You and Your Network*. Fred said that when others deal with us in a mean and vicious way, in most cases it's not because they want to hurt us. It's far more likely that they are acting that way because *they* are hurting. Please understand that every obnoxious act is a cry for help. Recognizing and accepting this fact makes it much easier for us to take a calmer, more levelheaded approach to our functions as managers and as people.

It's Up to You

All of life is a series of choices, and what you choose to give life today will determine what life will give you tomorrow. You can choose to get drunk tonight, but when you do, you have chosen to feel miserable tomorrow. You can choose to light up a cigarette today, but when you do, you have chosen to die fourteen minutes early. You can choose to eat properly today, and when you do, you have chosen to be healthier tomorrow. You can choose to be overweight, or you can choose to work toward the right weight. You can choose to be happy, or you can choose to be sad.

For twenty-four years of my adult life, by choice I weighed over two hundred pounds. I say this because in my lifetime (at least since infancy), I have never *accidentally* eaten anything! Every bite is carefully planned and deliberately taken. I even set aside at least three times every day when I concentrate almost exclusively on taking those bites of food. When I choose to eat too much today, I have chosen to weigh too much tomorrow. In 1972 I *chose* not to be overweight and took the appropriate steps to reach and maintain a healthy weight. It was one of my better choices.

Never will I forget the night my wife (whom I affectionately call "the Redhead") and I were in our favorite ice cream parlor when a young man and his girlfriend walked in. He appeared to be about twenty-three or twenty-four years old. I gently nudged the Redhead and pointed out the couple, and the following dialogue took place.

Zig: "Do you see that couple?" The Redhead: "Yes, I do." Zig: "Wonder what happened to him." The Redhead: "What do you mean?" Zig: "Well, just look at him! He's been in some kind of accident. He's hurt!" The Redhead: "Aw, honey, he's not hurt! He's been to the barbershop." Zig: "You mean he paid money to look like *that*?" (In my lifetime, I've never seen a human being that badly mutilated from the ears up. It was awesome!) The Redhead: "Sure, honey! He's trying to be different and original, so he's chosen to imitate some rock star."

> Every obnoxious act is a cry for help.

Don't misunderstand; one of the things I love best about my country is the fact that we are free and can choose to look any way we please. The major point I wish to make is that when that young fellow chose to look that way, he had also chosen to eliminate 98 percent of all employment opportunities. For example, we could not consider hiring him at our company. He would be a total distraction, and we'd have to spend half our time just explaining him!

When a young person chooses to sit up late at night watching television or socializing, they have chosen to be sleepy in class the next day and, consequently, absorb less of the information they need to know in order to be successful in the competitive world in which they live. When we choose to be mean, nasty, and ornery toward other people, we have chosen to be treated in a mean, nasty, and ornery fashion by others. By the same token, when we choose to be thoughtful and considerate, we've chosen to be treated in a thoughtful and considerate manner. The list is endless, but the message is always the same: *You are free to choose, but the choices you make today will determine what you will be, do, and have in the tomorrows of your life.*

You can choose to take the necessary steps to help you succeed as a manager, or you can choose to ignore the experience of successful managers and take the consequences for you and your employees. We must teach our employees that they are responsible for their attitudes and their conduct and that in life, every choice we make, whether it is good or bad, has consequences! Once those consequences are thoroughly understood, it's easier to make the right choices. Common sense, gratitude, loyalty, and discipline are some of the right choices that Top Performers make.

> Every choice we make, whether it is good or bad, has consequences!

Back to the Airport

At the airline counter I had another choice. I could have ranted and raved and whooped and shouted and snorted and screamed and hollered. I could have made an absolute idiot of myself and embarrassed everybody around me as well as myself by screaming, "That's crazy! That's idiotic! I'm tired! I've been gone all week! My family wants to see me, and I want to see them! Who made this decision, anyway? Who runs this outfit?" Yes, I could have chosen that as the second reaction. *And the next flight still leaves at 6:05!*

Innocent or Guilty?

Question: Have you ever been heading for work, driving along, minding your own business, your mind in neutral, when suddenly somebody cuts sharply in front of you at an exit? You manage to avoid them by hitting your brakes full force while at the same time sounding your horn, shaking your fist at the offender, and even yelling, "You dummy! Why don't you watch what you're doing? I could've been killed and so could you!" Have you ever gotten upset about an incident like that and taken your anger to work, where you proceeded to tell everybody in earshot about this crazy driver who pulled in front of you and almost killed you? Did you wonder out loud why they allow people like that to get licenses? How could anybody have made such a foolish mistake? And you go on and on and on as you describe in angry terms how you almost got killed on the way to work. "They ought to keep people like that off the streets!" you declare with righteous indignation.

In the meantime, the person who committed the dastardly deed rides merrily on, completely oblivious to the fact that you even exist or that anything unusual has happened. And yet that person is in complete control of your life. They are in charge of your mind and your emotions. They are affecting your productivity, your relationships with others, even your very future, and (once more) *they don't even know you exist*! One of our greatest gifts is the ability to choose the way we think, act, or feel, and the ultimate personal put-down is when we permit someone like the above-mentioned driver to take charge of our lives and our attitudes.

Think with me for a moment. If you are the way you are because "when your mother was pregnant with you, she was scared by a runaway horse, and consequently you have been scared of big brown animals ever since," if you are the way you are because they "snatched you off the potty too soon," if you are the way you are because of someone else, then here's what you do: You take the person who's responsible for the way you are to the psychologist, the psychologist will treat that person, and *you* will get better! See how crazy that is? If you fall and break your arm, you don't send a friend to the doctor to have their arm set. You don't even send the one who pushed you! You go yourself—you take personal responsibility! It's the same for your mental and emotional health. You must accept personal responsibility.

Yes, I know that *your past is important*, but as important as it is, according to Dr. Tony Campolo, *it is not nearly as important as the way you see your future*. Here's why: The way you see your future determines your thinking today. Your thinking today determines your performance today, and your performance in the todays of your life determines your future. This is especially true when you learn to respond and not react to life's daily challenges.

It's been said before and it will be said again: You cannot change the past, but your future is spotless. You can write on it what you will. In order to do so, however, you need to learn to *respond* to the positive *and* the negative. Fortunately, you have far more control than you realize. For example, all of us have on occasion been guilty of saying, "He/She makes me so mad!" That simply is not so. As a wise man said, you can't stir the soup unless there's some soup in the pot to stir. Nobody can make you *act* mad unless there is already some mad in you. Mad reactions are *learned* behaviors, and consequently they can be *unlearned*.

This is a key principle. Top Performers know that they cannot keep adding positive new information without burying some of the old input.

You can watch a person go about their daily activities for days or weeks and learn a great deal about them. However, you can watch someone under adverse circumstances for five minutes and

> The lights are always on and the camera is always rolling.

see whether they have learned to respond or to react. Actually, you can learn more about that person in a few minutes under trying conditions than you can in days of just watching them involved in daily activities.

Your response—or reaction—to the negative reveals what's inside of you. It exposes your heart and shows the kind of person you really are. The problem is that most people have a tendency to react instead of respond and to blame everything and everybody for their difficulties in life.

Question: Do You Respond or React?

I've been beating the bushes a long time, but I seldom hear anyone make a habit of blaming someone else for their success. They don't say, "It's all my manager's fault for spending a lot of extra time with me and making me study, drill, and prepare. My manager's the reason

I'm successful today." Most of the time we don't even say, "It was my spouse's or parents' fault. They kept after me night and day until I did what was necessary, and that's the reason I've been successful." No, most of us have a tendency to blame somebody else for our difficulties but keep appropriate credit for our success to ourselves. What about you? Do you *respond* to the negative and make it better, or do you *react* to the negative and make it worse?

To be a Top Performer, you must make the proper choices. Now if you have never had instruction on how to respond positively or what people do to become Top Performers, then you have a built-in excuse. But wait a minute! I'm not going to let you hang your hat on that excuse. Together we are going to look at *how*, *what*, *who*, *why*, *when*, and *where* to make the proper choices so that you can get the most out of yourself and others! The following story from Krish Dhanam is a tremendous example of responding or reacting.

Years ago, I found myself standing outside a hotel, waiting for the shuttle that would take me to the airport. It had been a successful trip. Looking back on that moment, in which I felt grateful for the opportunities that exist in America and my career in general, you could say I was riding higher than a kite, and nothing was going to bring me down that day.

The shuttle driver was running late and, deciding to be proactive, I picked up my own bags and placed them in the shuttle bus that was standing in front of the hotel. My thought process was fairly simple. If I put the bags in, we would save that amount of time when the driver arrived, and we could be on our way.

If you look at a picture of me, you will notice that I look different. My ethnic looks, coupled with the traveling gear I was loading into the shuttle bus, led to some mistaken assumptions by my fellow travelers. You could say that they mistook me for a baggage handler who could not speak English, as is evidenced by their subsequent actions.

The first random act of ignorance was committed by the woman standing next to me as she beckoned me to repeat the process she had seen me undertake. Simply put, she used nonverbal commands to ask me to place her luggage in the shuttle. I obliged and then returned to my rightful spot and continued the wait.

The next act of ethnic profiling was committed by a gentleman who suggested I do the same with his luggage. Once again I obliged. This time, however, I needed to make a statement of my own. Instead of reacting, I remembered Zig Ziglar once telling me that in life you need to respond, because the lights are always on and the camera is always rolling.

As a training ambassador for Ziglar Inc., my obligation was to represent my company with the highest standards possible. Yelling at those people that day would have satisfied me more than anything I can imagine. I am an educated, hardworking, honest, tax-paying citizen, and these people assumed I was a baggage handler—many of whom, I must tell you, are also educated, hardworking, honest, tax-paying citizens. That was kind of presumptuous, if I do say so myself, and most folks would have reacted, but I chose to respond. So with a smile, I extended my open hand to each of them and netted nearly four dollars—what a country!

The reason for telling about something that was painful at the time it happened is twofold. First, it is to show that responding was the best thing to do of all possible options available to me at that time. Second, it is to share with you what the man said to me when I boarded the shuttle and he realized that he had made a mistake. He simply said, "I wish all my employees had your disposition." Years later as I continue to participate in the process of categorizing Top Performance principles, I am grateful that a cooler head prevailed that day, and in my heart I know that I emerged a greater victor than the two people who got caught up in perceptions and mistaken assumptions.

---------------- **PERFORMANCE PRINCIPLES** ----------------

1. Regardless of your past, tomorrow is a clean slate.

2. Every obnoxious act is a cry for help.

3. Don't waste time placing blame; fix the cause!

4. The choices you make today will determine what you will be, do, and have in the tomorrows of your life.

5. Top Performers learn to make the proper choices.

6. Top Performers know that when they continuously add new concepts and ideas into their minds, they are burying some of the archaic ideas already in place.

3

Causing Others
to *Want* Your Leadership

Leadership is the art of getting someone else to do something
that you want done because he wants to do it.

Dwight D. Eisenhower

I thoroughly enjoy promoting my books, but the schedule is generally
hectic. Over the years the media, with few exceptions, have been extremely
kind to me. Bookstores have been delighted to sponsor autograph parties
because they usually sell lots of books, which is why they are in business.
I had been out late promoting my book *Secrets of Closing the Sale* in New
York and didn't arrive at my next destination, a beautiful hotel in Houston, Texas, until 2:30 a.m. I was really excited, since I had experienced a
truly incredible day where *everything* had gone exactly right. Wonderful
interviews, friendly people, lots and lots of sales. And my first interview
the next day wasn't until 11:00 a.m.

A Sense of Humor Will Help

As I approached the desk to register, a quick glance at the night clerk told
me things had not been going well for her. Her facial expression indicated

37

she not only had lost her last friend but had also had some M&Ms melt in her hand, and she might even have received some junk mail with the postage due. Despite her melancholy countenance, I enthusiastically approached the registration desk, and the following exchange took place.

Zig: "Good morning, how ya doin'?" Night Clerk: "Oh, I suppose I'll make it." Zig: "I bet you not only make it, I bet you are going to win!" Night Clerk: "Well, you certainly feel good though it's so late!" Zig: "Yes, I do. When I woke up this morning, I knew I was ahead of the game, because *some* people did not wake up this morning." (She *almost* smiled at that.) Night Clerk: "Well, I suppose that's the best way to look at it." Zig: "It definitely is." Night Clerk: "I suppose so, but I need to get you to fill out our registration slip." As I handed the slip back to her, she said, "Now I need a major credit card." Fortunately, I was able to comply with her request, so I handed her this version of a truly major credit card.

When she saw the card, she burst out laughing and even demonstrated some real enthusiasm as she said, "You know, I'm delighted you came along. I definitely feel better—but I'm going to need some other form of identification."

MAJOR CREDIT CARD

Good for One Enthusiastic Laugh from Highly Intelligent Individuals with a Keen Sense of Humor and a Real Zest for Life! (Or one small frown from the real sourpusses of the world.)

_____
Signature

Ziglar Training Systems

2009 Chenault Drive, Suite 100 • Carrollton, TX 75006 • 972-233-9191
www.ZiglarTraining.com/small business

With that comment I turned the card over, and when she saw what you are now looking at, she almost did the proverbial roll on the floor:

SOME OTHER FORM OF IDENTIFICATION

This certifies and verifies that the bearer is an honest, sincere, dedicated, hardworking, bill-paying, flag-waving, God-fearing, family-loving individual whom I unhesitatingly recommend for unlimited cash purchases!

Zig Ziglar

Question: Do you think she was a better employee the rest of her shift? I'll answer it for you. You betcha! Question: Why? Answer: A change of attitude.

I include this little episode because I believe that in our high-intensity world, a sense of humor can play a major role in our physical and emotional health. Humor helps us relate to others and will help make them want to know us, to please us, and to follow our leadership and direction.

Actually, I believe management goes beyond leadership, because management is that special kind of leadership in which the goals of the organization must be combined with the goals of the individual for the good of both. If the individual's goals are more important than the organizational goals or are in conflict with organizational goals, the organization will suffer. Similarly, if organizational goals overshadow individual goals or are in conflict with individual goals, the person will suffer. Excellent managers of people cause others to *want* to channel their energies for the maximum benefit of both.

This obviously applies whether we are talking about an office, an athletic team, a church, a home, or any situation where two or more people are gathered with a potentially common interest. Our objective must be to foster this common interest and be sure that individual and organizational goals complement each other as much as possible.

Leaders Deserve—and Get—Cooperation

No matter how brilliant or how technically capable you are, you won't be effective as a leader unless you gain the *willing cooperation of others*. For example, let's think together about the number of people you can really "force" to cooperate. Eliminate the boss, who is over you. You can't force those at your level because they are equal in authority. You can't even force a subordinate to obey without the subordinate filing a complaint, quitting, or developing so much resentment that their output will suffer directly or indirectly. Realistically, if you have a subordinate who always agrees, watch out! That person probably lacks self-starting qualities or the ability to think for themselves, or both. *Remember, cooperation, like leadership, is not getting the other person to do what you want. Rather, it means getting them to want to do what you want.* And there's a great deal of difference by the addition of this one word—*want*.

True cooperation generally depends on certain feelings that have been established over a period of time. It's the responsibility—and opportunity—of the leader to understand and develop these deeper feelings and then to work *with* them rather than against them. Now let's look at some basic rules and thoughts for getting cooperation. You succeed in getting cooperation by giving your people DOSES of leadership—leadership that is Dynamic, Organized, Sensitive, Effective, and Strong-willed. The following examples were collected by Krish Dhanam as he interacted over the years with the people mentioned.

Dynamic. Leaders who are dynamic understand that they need fluidity in their style of leadership so as to be able to get along with everyone. Leadership involves getting along with and getting maximum production from everyone, including those with whom we disagree. This flexibility is what dynamic leaders possess that allows them to guide their teams through both the good times and the tough ones. Paul Horgen, who was president and CEO of IBM's Credit Union in Rochester, Minnesota, when this book was written, exemplifies this trait. At the time when the popularity of savings and loans was not at an all-time high, he was using his dynamism to guide his own organization through some remarkable periods of growth. When Paul attended one of our events in Dallas, he proved that even though he was already a leader in his field, he was still keen on being a student who could continue on the path of learning as he improved himself to be a better leader for his people.

Organized. Organized leaders carefully plan their projects and choose the time and place when their ideas are most likely to be accepted. Once the ideas are organized, they present them in a clear and concise way. When I first wrote this, Kevin Small was president of INJOY, a leadership training and development company in Atlanta. Designed to deliver the teachings of leadership luminary John Maxwell, INJOY and its counterpart, Maximum Impact, have done remarkably well in assembling some of the brightest leadership minds to reach thousands across the country at the same time. Kevin is one of the most organized and effective people I know. I first met Kevin when he was organizing the logistics for John Maxwell seminars in the early '90s. His meteoric rise to the head of that organization is a testimony to his belief in the importance of being organized. Kevin is truly a Top Performer.

Sensitive. Sensitive leaders know that to get real cooperation they must understand that they do not have all the answers. In all probability, the facts and figures required to make a decision may lie with others. Leaders who are sensitive to the feelings of others can get cooperation from those around them.

Effective. Learning to look at things from the perspective of others is a sign of effectiveness. Successful leaders are very rarely comfortable. Successful leaders are expected to be effective. The difference between comfort and effectiveness is called growth, and growth is what separates Top Performers from the rest of the pack.

> Make sure your leaders are the right people with the right vision at the right time.

Strong-willed. Successful leaders are fair but firm. They understand that other people are also right at times and are entitled to have their opinions and ideas heard. Strong-willed leaders learn how to pass all the concerns of an organization through the foundational filter of vision and mission. They know how to determine if an idea, opinion, or strategy lines up with the goals and dreams of an organization.

Why Should Anyone Want to Follow You?

I hope that once you get past the attention-grabbing value of this question, you can turn your interest and attention to the point: Have you taken a personal inventory of your strengths as a manager? Come on, now, there must be some reason why you have your position. This is not the time for false modesty. Try to recall the positive statements you have heard from others. The fact that we have trouble remembering positive reinforcement is a terrible indictment of our society and should emphasize to each of us the importance of sincerely pointing out the good we see in others. However, now is the time to honestly face some facts about yourself and your future as a manager of people. Look at areas such as planning, organization, communication, listening, decision making, delegation, and motivation. Before we can go any further, right here and now list at least ten *strengths* you have as a manager of people.

Significant Reasons Others Should Want to Follow Me

1. _____
2. _____
3. _____
4. _____
5. _____
6. _____
7. _____
8. _____
9. _____
10. _____

Regardless of the length or strength of the list you made, you can become even more effective as a manager of people. John D. Rockefeller stated, "I will pay more for the ability to deal with people than any other ability under the sun." To cause others to *want* our leadership and management, we must become experts in the kind of people skills to which Mr. Rockefeller was referring. According to Ralph Waldo Emerson, "*Our chief want is someone who will inspire us to be what we know we could be.*" Dan Rather, past *CBS Evening News* anchor, took Emerson's idea a step further when he said, "The dream begins with a teacher who believes in you, who tugs and pushes and leads you to the next plateau, sometimes poking you with a sharp stick called 'truth.'" As a manager, you must embody all that these men are speaking of and more. If this sounds like an overwhelming task, it is not. Actually, becoming an expert in the people business can be very simple. I did not say "easy"; nothing in life is easy. But managing people should not—*must* not—be made complex.

Krish Dhanam knows better than most what it takes to find the right leader. Here are his insights on the topic.

When I joined the Zig Ziglar organization in 1991, Bryan Flanagan was my sales manager. I was recruited away from a job in the telecom-

munications industry and came with a lot of excitement. Up until that time in my career, I had been conditioned to do what was expected of me and no more. I did not fully understand the concept of going above and beyond the call of duty. My probation period was ninety days, and my compensation was tiered to reflect the satisfactory completion of preset goals along the way. When the ninety-day deadline came on me, I was still shy of the performance expectations set for me by what amounted to about six hundred dollars. I approached Bryan for assistance, not knowing what direction the meeting would take. Bryan encouraged me to go back and give it my all, as the day was still young. I did accordingly, but by early afternoon I had only sold about seventy additional dollars, leaving me a good deal shy of my goal.

Bryan Flanagan is a leader people like to follow because of his random acts of kindness. That day Bryan gave me a lead to follow up on. The decision maker of a North Dakota automobile dealership had wanted Bryan's services but was apprehensive about the financials involved. Because Bryan agreed to accept the engagement for a lot less than his standard fee, I procured the contract, reached my goal, and continued my career with the company. That day Bryan's Top Performance led to the salvaging of my career. Bryan and I continue to be good friends, as is evident from our work on this project and the numerous training sessions we've conducted together.

When you do something out of the ordinary, you never know what the impact of those actions will be. You may even become the kind of leader others want to follow. Top Performers see something in others that others may not see in themselves. In my eyes Bryan Flanagan is one such Top Performer.

Do You Rush to Judgment?

A family counselor once said that what most married people want is a spouse they can look up to but also one who will not look down on them. A manager's or leader's team members want *exactly* the same thing. Someone they can truly look up to—but someone who does not look down on them. This is the goal all managers should strive for in dealing with their people. This next story out of my own book of life makes the point quite well.

Several years ago, while on my way to a small town in Ohio for a speaking engagement, I had to stop in Pittsburgh to make a connection. I had a little over an hour on my hands, so as I walked toward the connecting gate, I was in no particular hurry. Two young men had a booth and were shining shoes.

One of the guys was "Mr. Personality"—outgoing, jovial, pleasant— the kind of guy who could brighten up any party. The other was the exact opposite—somber, quiet, absolutely nonexpressive. He was "just there." I wanted "Mr. Personality" to shine my shoes, but he was still working on another customer when I arrived, and the quiet young man was available, so I had no other option.

As I stepped up into the chair, I cheerfully greeted the young man with, "How ya doin'?" He simply looked at me as if I did not exist and said absolutely nothing. I could not help but think that his behavior was certainly strange for somebody who was working with the public and who, to a large degree, depended on tips for his income. However, since I am an incurable optimist, I started rationalizing that in all probability I had gotten the one who was the best at what I wanted done—namely, shining shoes.

As the young man applied the saddle soap to clean the shoes, I immediately noticed he was very meticulous—extremely careful not to get any of the soap on my socks or my pant leg—and I was pleased with that. As he dried the shoes, I again noticed how extraordinarily careful he was and how efficiently he worked. By the time he finished applying the polish, I was convinced I had come out ahead by getting him. He was very thorough and careful. As a matter of fact, he's the only guy I've ever seen who looked around at the back of my shoes to make certain he was applying polish everywhere.

When he started brushing the shoes, it was obvious that he was using the artist's touch. He was very good, and I was getting more enthusiastic all the time. When he applied the cloth to the leather, he had to use a little pressure to get the high gloss he wanted. It was at this point that, for the first time, I really *looked* at the young man. Since the enthusiastic kid in the next stand had finished, there was no one in the other chair, so things were extremely quiet for the first time, and I heard an almost inaudible "uh-uh-uh." At this point I realized the young man had a disability.

As you can well imagine, I felt like about two cents. Here I, in my high-and-mighty judgmental way, had decided I was going to "honor" this young man by "letting" him shine my shoes! In my own mind, I was even going to be bighearted and give him a nice tip—*if* he was pleasant, courteous, gracious, outgoing, and also gave me a magnificent shine!

Needless to say, it was a very humbling experience, and this young man got the biggest tip I've ever given to anybody for shining my shoes. I've often thought about the young man's parents and what a magnificent job they had done in teaching him to use his abilities. They had to be good people and outstanding managers as well.

As managers, our job is to further the abilities our people have and then lead them to use those abilities productively. As Fred Smith said, a manager "is not a person who can do the work better than his men; he is a person who can get his men to do the work better than he can." In many cases our employees have much more talent than we realize they have. It's also true that some people are a little slower than others at developing and manifesting their abilities. I think of people like artist Grandma Moses, who was seventy-eight before she started painting in earnest; Albert Einstein, who was four years old before he could walk or talk; Thomas Edison, who was considered "slow and dumb"; George Westinghouse, who was labeled "impractical" and "dull" and was asked to leave college because his teachers didn't think he could make it—and yet he was awarded a patent for the rotary steam engine before he was twenty!

The point I'm making with this is—or should be—obvious. Most people have considerable ability, often undeveloped, that is not always immediately noticeable. Many others, like the young man who shined my shoes, are more than willing to use what they've got to do a marvelous job. As managers, we need to be ever alert to find and develop whatever talent is available in our company or department.

A Formula for Success

I think you will agree that the responsibility for your unit—whether it is you and one other person or you and one hundred other people—is to function together for a common cause or purpose. Unquestionably, the

45

1984 Olympics held in Los Angeles were a great triumph, and one of the primary reasons was Peter Ueberroth, the manager in charge. According to many of those who worked closely with him, Mr. Ueberroth was successful because he made everyone believe they were involved in a cause that was bigger than the individual. The way he involved everyone in his (and their) cause was by using excellent people skills. He developed a team spirit and had everyone working together for the same end result. You can do the same thing with smaller or larger units by understanding this simple formula for success.

Much has been written and said about team effort. It's important for the family, for the athletic team, and for the workplace. Once a friend of mine was discussing a basketball team for which his son played. The team was functioning quite well early in the season. There were no superstars on board, but they had learned considerable discipline and a series of plays that were enabling them to beat teams that actually had greater individual talent. They had a good record. Then two guys who had been ineligible regained their eligibility and joined the team at the change of semesters. As individuals, these two guys were bigger, stronger, and faster than the other team members, and they were better shooters. Unfortunately, they did not have the discipline, nor did they know the plays. The net result was that though they had the talent, they actually were liabilities instead of assets to the team. Important point: They were liabilities because the coach did not have the courage to keep them on the bench until they learned the plays and developed the discipline to function as team members instead of individual talents. That coach (manager) let down himself, his team, his supporters, and the two individuals. The opposite behavior was witnessed in the performance of the Seattle Mariners baseball team in the 2001–2002 season. After losing superstars Ken Griffey Jr., Randy Johnson, and Alex Rodriguez, the Mariners played as a team and won a record 116 games in the regular season.

As managers, we frequently have similar situations arise in which individuals may have great talent and ability, but because of certain personality traits, annoying habits, or refusal to function as part of the team, they become liabilities instead of assets. The most important function a manager has is to bring the individuals together as a team—in other words, to make them "gel."

In athletics we often hear coaches talk about team spirit. They sell athletes on the importance of playing together for a common cause: *winning*! One of the catchwords that coaches use to describe unity is *gel*. They will say that the offense is just beginning to gel or that to be successful the defense must gel. Of course, they are talking about playing *together* and not as individuals, putting the objectives of the team ahead of personal gain so that when the team wins there will be great gain for each member of the team.

Some reporters have spelled *gel* with a *J* because of the television commercials about Jell-O, but actually *gel* means "to congeal or come together." For our purposes, let's take these three letters and use them as an acrostic to remind us how to be experts in the business of managing people. The next three chapters will take each of these letters individually and give specific instructions on how we can use this formula to become Top Performers.

————————— **PERFORMANCE PRINCIPLES** —————————

1. A sense of humor is vital to good leadership.
2. Common goals plus a common cause equal greater success.
3. Cooperation must be earned, not demanded.
4. Face up to your strengths as well as your weaknesses.
5. Not all resources are obvious; great managers find and develop available talent.
6. Playing as a team increases the odds of winning.

4

Look for the Good

How far you go in life depends on your being tender with the young, compassionate with the aged, sympathetic with the striving, and tolerant of the weak and the strong. Because someday in life you will have been all of these.

George Washington Carver

GOODFINDERS
EXPECT THE BEST
LOYALTY

The *G* in our GEL formula stands for *Goodfinders*—those who are experts in Top Performance learn to look for the good in each person they manage.

Andrew Carnegie said, "No man can become rich without himself enriching others." He went on to live this philosophy, as evidenced by the forty-three millionaires he had working for him. A reporter interviewing Mr. Carnegie asked how he was able to hire that many millionaires. Mr. Carnegie patiently explained that the men were not millionaires when they came to work for him but had become millionaires by working for him. When the reporter pursued the line of questioning as to how he was able to develop these men to the point they were worth that much money, Mr. Carnegie said, "When you work with people, it is a lot like mining for gold. . . . When you mine for gold, you must literally move tons of dirt to find a single ounce of gold. However, you do not look for the dirt—you look for the gold!"

It works the same way when you want to develop people to their full potential. You must look for the gold (the good), and when you find it, you nurture it and bring it to fruition. Another wise man, Benjamin Disraeli, expressed it this way: "The greatest good you can do for another is not just share your riches, but to reveal to him his own."

Bill Hewlett, one of the founders of Hewlett-Packard, said, "Our policy flows from the belief that men and women want to do a good job, a creative job, and that if they are provided with the proper environment they will do so." Since people want to do a good job, why shouldn't we point out their success as it occurs?

The next illustration from my childhood tells about an effective method of dealing with your people when they don't do their jobs as effectively or professionally as they can and should. As you read this, I encourage you to remember some wise words from Dr. Norman Vincent Peale: "The trouble with most of us is that we would rather be ruined by praise than saved by criticism."

Criticize the Performance—Not the Performer

Some of you will recognize the following story from my book *Raising Positive Kids in a Negative World*, but it so vividly makes the point that I want to repeat it here. When I was a small boy down in Yazoo City, Mississippi, things were pretty tight during those Depression years, and everybody had to work smarter and harder. As a leader and as a manager, I honestly believe my mother would rate close to the top despite her fifth-grade education.

Dad died when I was five years old and left six of us too young to work. Remember now, this was in the heart of the Depression, and things were tough for everyone. We survived because we had a very large garden and three milk cows. I was milking and working in the garden by the time I was eight years old and, for what it's worth, let me interject the fact that cows don't "give" milk—you have to fight for every drop!

There were two things we always knew when Mother gave us an assignment. Number one, we knew what she *ex*pected (our very best). Number two, we knew she was going to *in*spect to make certain she got what she *ex*pected.

I'll never forget my first solo assignment in the garden. On this particular day, because my mother was also a good teacher, she showed me exactly what I needed to do to hoe those beans properly. When she finished her lesson, she pointed to three rows of beans—which were about three and a half miles long (well, would you believe three?). But to an eight-year-old boy they looked more like ten! Anyhow, Mama instructed me that when I finished I was to call her so she could inspect what I had done. When I finally finished, I called her for the inspection. As she looked the job over, she did what she always did when she was not pleased with something. She folded her hands behind her back, ducked her head, cocked it slightly to the right, and started that little left-to-right head-shaking motion that I knew all too well. As she was doing this, I asked her what was the matter. She smiled and said, "Well, son, it looks like you're going to have to lick this calf over."

Now in the corporate world that may seem like a strange phrase, but in those days in rural Mississippi it simply meant that what I had done was unsatisfactory and I was going to have to do it over again. Obviously, I knew what she was saying, but—hopeful for an escape—I smiled and said, "Mama, I wasn't botherin' the calf—I was hoeing those beans!" With this my mother chuckled and said, "Well, son, what I mean is this: For most boys this would be perfectly all right. But you're not most boys. You're *my* son, and my son can do better than this."

What Mother had done was extremely wise. *She had criticized the performance* because it badly needed criticism, *but she had praised the performer* because he needed the praise.

Effective management, whether in athletics, education, family, or business, is measured by your effectiveness in managing your personnel to get maximum productivity and benefits for all. To accomplish this objective there are two things that great managers always do. Number one, they always *ex*pect every member of the team to do their best; and number two, they always *in*spect to make certain they get what they *ex*pected. (There is almost nothing as demotivating to a subordinate as having a completed project ignored or taken for granted after heart and soul have been poured into that project.)

Question: Suppose your inspection reveals that the project is either unsatisfactory or not up to the standards you feel that individual is capable of attaining. Do you "brag on" the individual or "fuss at" them? Answer: Neither. To brag on any project that represents less than a person's capability is to encourage mediocrity, and the corporate world is already oversupplied with that commodity. You owe that person more than that. To fuss at them or to be harshly critical could well destroy the subordinate's confidence and stifle their initiative for future projects. You also owe that person and your company more than that. Question: So what do you do? Answer: You use a page from my mother's notebook. Criticize the performance—not the performer!

Effective leadership demands that kind of approach. Extend the hand of encouragement to the person while making it clear that you expect—even demand—that they use their ability for maximum results. In short, have that person reaching for more, but do it without challenging or questioning their worth as an individual. Assure them that you *really* respect and appreciate their ability—and that's why work that is not consistent with their ability is unacceptable.

The ABCs of Management

Ken Blanchard has worked with several other outstanding authors to compile a series of "one minute" books. These books are easy to read and have really simplified some foundational concepts. Dr. Blanchard worked with Dr. Robert Lorber on a book called *Putting the One Minute Manager to Work*. In this outstanding book, these men identify the ABCs of management and reveal some startling facts.

A = Activators: what a manager does *before* performance
B = Behavior: performance, what someone says or does
C = Consequences: what a manager does *after* performance

For example, according to Blanchard and Lorber, "Most people think activators have a greater influence on performance than consequences. And yet, only 15–25% of what influences performance comes from activators like goal setting, while 75–85% of it (behavior) comes from consequences like praising and reprimands." What happens *after* a person does something has more impact than what happens *before*! To use another "one minute" phrase, "Catch them doing something right!" If you can catch people doing something well, no matter how small it may seem, and positively reinforce them for doing it, they will continue to grow in a positive direction.

Does this mean that we are to ignore the mistakes of those for whom we are responsible? Of course not, but there is a correct way to handle the errors or deal with the person whose overall job performance is unsatisfactory or begins to slip. I will address these issues later in this chapter. For the moment, however, let me simply state that the *best managers make finding the good in others a priority*. Too many managers do exactly the opposite.

Action Often Precedes the Feeling

Most of us, in our daily managerial duties, don't feel like goodfinders. As a matter of fact, we often become the exact opposite and function in a role similar to school disciplinarians or police detectives. Den Roossien, past executive vice president of the Zig Ziglar Corporation, used a slightly different technique that I would like to recommend to you. Den was responsible for the daily operations of our company and was our chief financial officer. He came from an accounting background, and he would be the first to tell you that people skills are not emphasized in accounting courses and that he really had to study and work on this area of his professional expertise. One technique Den used while he was with our company that I believe you will find extremely helpful was to keep a running list of the minute, and sometimes seemingly insignificant, successes of the people who fell under his responsibility. The list may have included things such as staying late to see that a rush package got out on time or arriving early to set up chairs for our Monday morning devotions—the little things that make the big difference. He would verbally point out the fact that he appreciated the effort—*as soon as possible after the behavior.* This follows one of the most important rules of positive reinforcement: *It should be immediate.* In addition, he wrote the behavior down in a notebook so that at the end of the year, or at quarterly review times, he could share with our people-building team a series of seemingly inconsequential behaviors that worked together to dramatically impact the bottom line of our company.

The time Den invested in keeping notes was really worthwhile when compared to the goodwill and positive reinforcement benefits. Sure, it takes discipline to remember and follow through, but Den was committed to a disciplined approach when it came to the factors and procedures that positively impacted our company. Discipline and organization were both involved, and fortunately, Den had fully developed both characteristics (there was even a persistent rumor that he was so well organized he periodically proofread the Xerox copies).

Did he always *feel* like doing this? Certainly not, but action often precedes the feeling. When it comes to giving positive feedback, we sometimes may not *feel* like doing so; that is why it is even more important that we do so immediately. If griping and complaining can become a habit, why can't goodfinding become a habit? One reason is that we have not been trained to look for the good. Another obvious reason is that we don't fully comprehend the motivational impact a word of encouragement can have on an employee or coworker.

There are two things you must remember. Number one: *The compliment must be sincere.* If not, the people you work with will know it faster than you do, and you will lose all credibility. Number two: *You cannot follow every compliment with a correction.* When this happens, the technique is viewed as manipulative because *it is.* This results in a double-lose situation in the long run.

How do you feel when you get an email or phone call and the boss says, "I want to see you *right away!*" Ninety-five out of one hundred people get that "glitch" in their stomachs and that *What did I do wrong?* thought in their minds. We have been trained to expect the worst in that type of situation. However, imagine that your boss is the kind of people manager who looks for the good and normally compliments you. When you get the call, you actually look forward to your time together—it's a whole new mind-set. The real question is: How do you want your workers, friends, spouse, children, and others to feel when they get the call that you want to see them?

A Tool for Written Feedback

Some people really do have trouble verbalizing feedback; but have no fear, because this is an acquired or learned skill. However, until you learn the skill, you need a practical tool for feedback. Here is a great one for you, whether you have excellent verbal skills or are just learning. In our Ziglar seminars, we use a tool called the I LIKE . . . BECAUSE pad. Each participant is given a pad like the one shown in the illustration and asked to note things they like or appreciate about class members during the seminar. This is an original idea given to us by Bay City High School in Bay City, Texas. It has an enormous impact on seminar participants, as well as on numerous homes and businesses across America where it is used.

The I LIKE . . . BECAUSE pad teaches us to look for the good and causes us to point out the positives we see in others. The comments run from the simple, such as complimenting the way a person smiles, to the more complex ideas, showing deeper levels of appreciation.

When we first introduced the concept in our Born to Win seminar in Dallas, there was one participant who used his body language to express his obvious disapproval. He squirmed, turned to the side, folded his arms, crossed his legs, and in general said, "I'm not having any part of this silliness!" Well, our seminar facilitators watched this man's comments carefully as they distributed the sheets to the participants. The first day's comments were seldom more than a few words. On day two, his comments gradually got longer, and on day three he was filling up the front and back of the sheets. At the end of class, he stood up and said, "When these I LIKE . . . BECAUSE pads were introduced, I thought it was the silliest idea I had ever heard, but it's amazing how much you people have changed over the last few days!" Obviously, the people had changed because Born to Win really is a life-changing experience, but

```
┌─────────────────────────────────────┐
│                                     │
│   I Like _____   │
│   because_____    │
│   _____    │
│   _____    │
│   _____    │
│   _____    │
│                                     │
│        You Are a Winner!!!          │
│                                     │
└─────────────────────────────────────┘
```

even more obviously, this man had also changed because he was learning to look for the good in others.

We have a two-day seminar called Presentation Skills Training in which we coach people on their communication skills. Over the two days, the participants are recorded a dozen times and given private coaching and feedback on how they might improve their communication skills. In addition to American Airlines, DuPont, and others, world-famous Neiman Marcus department store had our instructors "in house" to train some of their key personnel. They liked the I LIKE concept, adapted it, and printed YOU ARE WHAT WE'RE FAMOUS FOR! on their pads. Under this great heading, they write their positive comments about their peers.

Does Anybody Ever Really Use Those Things?

Krish Dhanam tells this story about the I LIKE . . . BECAUSE comments:

A participant at one of our seminars wrote the following letter in which she shared hidden feelings of gratitude with people she may never meet, while claiming a victory that cannot be quantified. As is evident, the letter is written to my parents, who live in India. Embrace this letter personally and think of what it would mean to you if your parents received a letter thanking them for the job they did in raising you. Of the many things my father has said to me in praise and love, the thing he references most is the letter he received from total strangers thanking him for a job well done.

55

October 9, 1995

Dear Mr. and Mrs. Dhanam,

We have never met formally, but as a result of three days that my daughter and I spent in Dallas this past week, I feel as though we have met. We had the privilege of attending the Born to Win seminar that was given by Zig Ziglar and his wonderful staff. We first met your son Krish at a reception at Zig's house on Wednesday evening. In the course of becoming acquainted, he asked Kristen and me where we were from, and we told him we were from Wheeling, West Virginia. He got a look of surprise on his face and said that not only had he been there several times, his wife and son were there now! My reaction was of almost denial, as I thought he MUST be kidding, but he went on to describe things in Wheeling that only someone who had been there could know. Once I realized he was being truthful, I became very excited that there was someone there from our hometown (ask Krish, I probably embarrassed us both!). He went on to explain that Anila is related to Pam Parmar, who happens to be the physician of both my mother-in-law and sister-in-law! At this point, I KNOW I embarrassed us both because I was so excited. Little did I know that we would become quick friends, and he would have much to teach to all of us during Born to Win.

As the days at the seminar went on, Krish spent considerable time describing his childhood, decision to come to the United States, and the time since he arrived here in 1986. The most moving story to me personally involved the time when Krish and his brother had made some very cruel and hurtful statements to you, Mrs. Dhanam, regarding your level of schooling and intelligence—as well as your decision that was sparked by those comments to return to school and your ultimate success in that venture.

I mentioned in opening this letter that I feel as though I have met you. I say that because I am of the opinion that when a child is as tremendously successful as Krish is, there are parents with very strong ideals and values standing behind him. Krish is articulate and immensely funny (he almost killed me at lunch one day when he showed his wonderful sense of humor; unfortunately I had just taken a bite of food at the time and almost choked!).

But I think the best thing I like about Krish is the genuine concern and love he showed to each of the 160+ people who were at the seminar. He shared of himself, but he also did everything in his power to help us to understand and make a part of us the awesome message that Zig presents. I told Krish as I was leaving that I felt I had gained a lifetime friend when I met him.

When I meet someone as powerful as Krish who gives credit back to the parents that raised him, I always find myself wanting to say "thank you" to them. It is through your years of sacrifice, hard work, and most of all unconditional love that Krish has come to understand that he is a born winner, and he has gone on to believe so strongly in the message that we are ALL born to win that he set a goal to work for Zig Ziglar and tell as many people as he could that they, too, are born to win.

The entire Ziglar Corporation staff, but especially Krish, have given my daughter and me a gift that will last and influence our entire lives. I believe, as does Krish, that there are no coincidences in life; I believe it was meant to be that we were at the seminar last week. It could ultimately not have happened without you, Mr. and Mrs. Dhanam, and Kristen and I both thank you from the bottom of our hearts.

Very fondly yours,
Debbie and Kristen

Mentoring is one of the most significant components of leadership. How much of an impact could you make on the life of someone who respects you if you were to write such a letter to him or her? How would you feel if someone you impacted wrote such a letter to you or to someone you respect and admire? Feedback for a job well done can come in many forms. Personalizing the feedback that is given to someone brings out the human side of leadership. In this day of corporate mistrust and financial scandals, how much more respected would the leaders be if the people who followed them could produce such examples of recognition and reward?

In my own career at Ziglar Inc., the testimonials from the clients mean a lot, but what means even more is the personalized, handwritten validation by Zig Ziglar, telling me that he is proud of me and that he is not surprised in the least that our clients are satisfied with my performance.

Krish isn't the only one who enjoys I LIKE . . . BECAUSE comments. Laurie Magers is my executive assistant and one of the most efficient people you will ever meet. In over twenty-five years of working together, I think Laurie has made three mistakes (and two of those were my fault!). The error she probably felt worst about was forgetting to tell me (again) about a television interview. You can imagine how bad she felt, and despite the fact that I pointed out that this was no major catastrophe and that it was at least 50 percent my fault, she was feeling very down for the biggest part of that day.

The next day when Laurie arrived at work, I LIKE . . . BECAUSE notes were hanging from the air conditioner vent above her desk and in a few other prominent places. Some of her friends at the office had noticed that she was down, found out why, and decided to do something to cheer her up. Someone had written, "I like Laurie because she can leap over a tall building with her computer under her arm!" and someone else wrote, "I like Laurie because she types at the speed of light!" And there were others who said, "I like Laurie because she is always willing to listen!" or, "I like Laurie because she is the most conscientious person in the Zig Ziglar Corporation!" Laurie was literally moved to tears by the thoughtfulness and encouragement of her fellow employees. And talk about motivated— man alive, you should have seen her productivity! She was back to normal in no time flat. The thoughtfulness of others, the fact that others were willing to look for the good and then point it out, helped Laurie through a difficult time.

Now if you are having a little trouble with the concept, this probably means you are zeroing in on the wrong word. The key word on the sheet is not *like*. If that word bothers you, simply scratch it out and insert *appreciate* or *respect*. The key word is *because*! This word moves the concept out of the superficial and general into the sincere and specific.

All of the effective management books on the market today encourage us to give feedback to employees. Giving feedback successfully means pointing out *specific and observable behavior*. "I like John *because* he brought in the project on time and under budget!" Not, "I like John because he is a good employee." "I like Jane *because* she worked overtime for three straight days to finish an important project!" Not, "I like Jane because she works hard." Remember: *Catch them doing something right!* When you do, you build on what's right instead of what's wrong.

Unless you have written or received an I LIKE . . . BECAUSE note, you cannot fully comprehend the impact of such a simple idea. Let me offer you a challenge right now: I want you to think of someone you need to tell that you appreciate, like (love), and/or respect them. Please think of that someone and make a commitment to yourself to stop reading and share a verbal or written I LIKE *immediately*!

Our course for schools is called the I CAN course.[1] It was developed by Mamie McCullough and is based on the principles in my first book, *See You at the Top*. One of the assignments we give the students is to go home and tell their parents they love them. You would be shocked, but your heart would also be warmed, if you could read some of the letters or listen in on some of the phone calls we get from parents in tears because, for the first time in their lives, a twelve- or fourteen-year-old child has said he or she loves them. Somebody in your life needs to know you appreciate them. You really need to make a commitment to yourself to do that today! Go ahead. The first time is by far the most difficult or awkward. In short order, because of the wonderful feedback, it will be fun and extremely rewarding.

Unusual Commodities

Love and respect are possibly the two most needed commodities in our society today. Unfortunately, they are also among the rarest. The reason they are unusual is that the *only* way we can *get* them is by *giving* them away. If you are not as loved or respected as you would like to be, you should give yourself a "gut" check and see if you are giving either of these items away. An important fact to remember is this: You cannot give away something you do not possess. In other words, the love and respect you should give to others is something you must have within yourself!

"There are high spots in all of our lives," wrote newspaper columnist George Matthew Adams, "and most of them have come about through encouragement from someone else. I don't care how great, how famous or successful a man or woman may be, each hungers for applause." If you will just recapture how good *you* feel after you have encouraged someone else, no other suggestion is necessary to persuade you to seize every opportunity to give encouragement. "Encouragement is oxygen to the soul," Adams continued. "Truly great work seldom comes from a worker without encouragement. No one ever *lived* long, happily or productively without it."

William James, the noted psychologist and philosopher, said without qualification: "The deepest principle in human nature is the craving to be appreciated." By helping to preserve the employee's or associate's self-respect, the effective leader brings that person closer to alliance by demonstrating a shared concern in a major area of personal values.

This approach is also desirable in dealing with opponents; it is *vital* in dealing with subordinates. The constant objective of higher-level executives must be to strengthen the competence and commitment of those who, in the last analysis, are responsible for implementing organizational objectives.

As Dr. Alan C. Filley writes in his important book *Interpersonal Conflict Resolution,* the portrait we draw of ourselves is a major determinant of how we behave. Various studies indicate that those with low self-esteem (1) are more likely to feel threatened in a situation, (2) are more vulnerable and dependent upon a power-laden situation, (3) have greater need for structure, (4) inhibit aggression, (5) are easily persuaded, and (6) yield more to group pressure than those with high self-esteem.

Not to be ignored is the importance of encouraging members of the group to respect each other. Acknowledging individual achievement should be done in ways that strengthen relationships not only between superior and subordinate but also between the subordinate and their peers. Praise given to one person should never be stated in terms that criticize other members of the group. And whenever the achievement was in fact accompanied by help from others, their contribution should also be acknowledged. Any other approach is likely to lead to group tensions rather than increased cooperation.

> You cannot give away something you do not possess.

Essentially, the key principle is the importance of *sharing the credit* both with and among subordinates. In a rare moment of self-revelation, Casey Stengel once said in perfectly articulate phrases: "Ability is the art of getting credit for all the home runs somebody else hits." But the surest way to keep the team from hitting home runs is to take the credit for yourself and never administer the athlete's salute—the pat on the base runner's behind.

But Isn't There a Time When We Must "Come Down On" Others?

Yes. Of course not all feedback is going to be positive. Some of you are thinking that I have overemphasized the concept of goodfinding—and you are partially correct. You really cannot say too much positive or find too much good in others, as long as each comment is sincere. The reason I have spent such an extended time writing about pointing out the good is that we (as a society in general) are so negligent in doing so. Now that the point has been emphasized, exactly how do we go about letting others know we are *not* pleased with their performance?

We start by really understanding what Jean Paul Richter meant when he said, "A man takes contradictions and advice much more easily than people think, only he will not bear it when violently given, even if it is well-founded. Hearts are flowers; they remain open to the softly falling dew, but shut up in the violent downpour of rain."

Bryan Flanagan holds the honor of being recognized by our staff as one of the most outstanding I LIKE . . . BECAUSE writers in our office. Everyone looks forward to getting feedback from Bryan because he is so kind and so specific. He carefully validates every compliment he gives. Many times he will give verbal feedback to support the written I LIKE and will do this in front of the supervisors of those he is complimenting—always sincerely.

Bryan also uses all the proper tools and techniques when it is time to give instructive feedback to those for whom he is responsible. On one occasion, Jim Savage, who at that time was Bryan's immediate supervisor, observed a "less than highly motivated" employee exiting Bryan's office. Naturally, he was interested in what happened.

Bryan told him, "You know, Jim, that young woman is one of the best workers we have in our division. She is at work on time every day and is more than willing to stay late when necessary. She is pleased to do just about anything that will benefit our organization. Why, just last month I asked her to take on a project that is somewhat outside her area of expertise and interest, and she not only took on the project, but she also performed extremely well. Actually, however, this project was what de-motivated her. The project I assigned took her off track from her normal duties, and since returning to these duties she has been less effective than before the project began. I simply pointed out that her productivity was not up to her usual standards and asked why—and then I listened. She shared her concerns, and during the conversation we were able to determine the specific behaviors and factors that were decreasing her productivity. With this information we were able to come up with a plan of action, which she agreed with and felt good about, to increase her productivity. I reminded her that she is not only a valuable employee but a valuable person as well. We also set a date when we would get together again to review the progress on our plan of action. She actually was relieved to discuss the concerns we both had, and while she was a little nervous about the meeting, she realized she needed direction and was glad I cared enough to give her the time and direction."

Bryan Flanagan is a role model for excellence in this particular scenario. I know you were picking out the key points as we went along, but let's go back together and be sure we have analyzed carefully.

1. *The feedback was given in private.* Nothing can be more devastating than public censure. Some managers are prone to tease or "dig" at an employee in front of others about a real concern as a way of hinting that they are displeased. All this does is destroy the seeds of trust between the people involved. *All* instructive or critical feedback must be given in private.

2. *The feedback was about specific, observable behavior.* The individual involved was never under personal attack. If there is to be criticism, it must pertain to the performance, *never* the performer.

3. *The feedback was immediate.* As soon as Bryan recognized the problem, he confronted the situation.

4. *Bryan asked questions and listened to the answers.* Rather than rushing to judgment, he asked questions for which, for the most part, he already had answers. He wasn't looking for the answers as much as he was looking for the employee's perspective on the answers. As a bonus, try closing your next instructive feedback

session with this question: "How do you think I feel about this meeting?" The answers will often surprise you and will generally give great insight about what has just transpired at your meeting.

5. *A cooperative plan of action was developed.* Bryan did not mandate what action was to be taken to correct the situation; rather, the two people involved discussed a mutually agreeable plan. The employee contributed and shared ownership of the plan.

6. *A date for a follow-up session was assigned to inspect to make sure Bryan got what he expected.* Too many excellent plans of action fall victim to the "tyranny of the urgent." With all good intentions, we try to get back to the employee, but things pop up and we forget. Establishing a specific date and setting an appointment creates a sense of urgency for the plan and helps prevent failure as well as hurt feelings from neglect.

7. *Praise was used throughout the session.* There is much debate about "sandwiching" criticism between praise. Some managers think they must start or end every session with praise. I will leave the decision on when to use praise up to you. However, to measure success, you must be able to answer this question affirmatively: "Did the person leave my presence with their self-esteem intact?" No one should ever leave an encounter with a manager doubting his or her personal value or self-worth.

To be a goodfinder we must often *teach* those for whom we are responsible to do something good. That is the objective of the instructive feedback session. The great managers give others instructions on how to be more successful—always giving direction within the ability level of the employee. The great managers do not ignore mistakes. Permissiveness is neglect of duty, for as Dr. Michael Mescon, former dean of the College of Business Administration, Georgia State University, said, "When a store clerk is rude, don't blame the clerk, blame the manager. The manager is ultimately responsible and accountable for actions of subordinates." If you will look for the good, point it out verbally and in writing, give instructive feedback in the manner outlined, and accept responsibility for those who answer to you, you are well on your way to becoming an excellent manager of people!

Marshall Field, American business leader and philanthropist, said, "Those who enter to buy support me. Those who come to flatter please me. Those who complain teach me how I may please others so that more will come. Only those hurt me who are displeased but do not complain. They refuse me permission to correct my errors and thus improve my service."

As leaders, we need to hitchhike on what Marshall Field said as a method for improving performance and assisting in the personal growth of our people. (Remember, if we only flatter the people, we are pleasing them. If pleasing them is all we do, we are participating in a conspiracy to prevent their further growth and opportunities for themselves as well as service to the company.)

A Positive Reminder

One of the most important aspects of motivating a workforce has to do with praise and recognition. That's the reason the I LIKE . . . BECAUSE approach is so effective. Before we close this chapter on goodfinding, let me share one last story that has a different twist.

A company sent four couples to one of our recent Born to Win seminars. At the end of the first day, they were tremendously motivated and excited about the I LIKE . . . BECAUSE idea. That evening they went to a late dinner at one of Dallas's most exclusive restaurants. They hit the jackpot. The food was exceptional and the service was superb. Their waiter was a professional with twenty-five years of experience, and over twenty of those years had been at that one restaurant. He was at their table when he needed to be, but he did not join the party. Friendly but not familiar. In short, to repeat myself, he was a pro.

The four couples were all personable and friendly and soon on a first-name basis with the waiter. The meal was particularly delicious and was greatly enhanced because of the waiter's gracious and effective service. The diners left him a 25 percent tip, which, in an expensive restaurant, is substantial. Each of the guests also left him an I LIKE . . . BECAUSE slip, detailing why they liked him. After they had made their exit and were about a hundred feet from the front door, they heard their waiter calling for them to wait a minute.

The waiter briskly walked up to them and, with the eight slips of paper in his hand, started to speak but broke down with emotion and for a moment or so literally could say nothing. When he finally regained his composure, he told the four couples that in his twenty-five years of being a waiter, this was far and away the most meaningful thing that had ever happened to him. Imagine!

The waiter was living proof of something my late friend and fellow speaker Cavett Robert used to say: "Three billion people on the face of the earth go to bed hungry every night, but four billion people go to bed every night hungry for a simple word of encouragement and recognition." It would be truly unfortunate if one of those people was your mother, father, child, or coworker who was in the midst of a difficult and challenging period in their life.

> Gratitude can be expressed in many ways, and the expression of gratitude is universal.

Do you think that with this kind of input this already effective waiter is going to be even more conscientious in his efforts? Do you think he benefited from the experience? Wouldn't you have loved to have been seated at the next table he served? Most important, who do you think were the biggest winners? Was it the waiter, who received the I LIKE . . . BECAUSE slips, or was it the eight individuals who wrote those notes? It doesn't take much imagination to answer that one, does it? I'm confident you agree that those who wrote the slips were the biggest winners.

That's what this concept is really all about. I would like to stress that we are talking about a *principle* and not a tactic. The Bible says, "Give and it shall be given unto you" (Luke 6:38). However, if we give or do for others with the expectation of having them do something for us, then our action is a tactic and is certain to either backfire or become entirely ineffective. However, if you buy into the concept that you can have everything in life you want if you will just help enough other people get what they want and then set about helping your people become more effective and more productive by giving them honest, sincere praise, not only will they benefit but you and your organization will also benefit tremendously. The magic thought is this: If it's a principle, it's a winner—if it's a tactic, it's a loser.

Don't forget that William James of Harvard said a deep need in human nature is the craving to be *appreciated*. When you, the manager, fill that need, you have taken a mammoth step toward becoming a more effective manager.

In 1996 I asked Krish Dhanam to become my replacement for the goal-setting segment of our two-day Born to Win seminar. I had watched him grow and felt he was ready. Later that year Krish presented me with a small, old-fashioned water pump made of brass. Many of you reading this know that the old-fashioned water pump has been my symbol of persistence for over three decades. Krish had bought it in a flea market in India and had it inscribed before he gave it to me.

> If it's a principle, it's a winner—if it's a tactic, it's a loser.

The words inscribed on the pump say something so universal that I thought it would be appropriate to share them with you. The inscription read as follows: "Gurudakshina—To a great teacher—Krish 1996." In Krish's native language, Telugu, the word *guru* means "teacher," and the word *dakshina* means "gift." Upon further inquiry Krish revealed to me that in India it was customary for the student to give a gift of appreciation to the teacher when the teacher informed the student that they were now ready.

By bringing me my own symbol of persistence all the way from India, Krish validated that gratitude and appreciation are universal concepts and that appreciation, love, and respect can and do cross both emotional and geographical boundaries.

PERFORMANCE PRINCIPLES

1. Look for the good in others.
2. Catch them doing something right.
3. Remember that action often precedes the feeling.
4. Seize the opportunity to share a sincere compliment.
5. Praise in public; censure in private.

5

Expect the Best

If you want to get the best out of a man, you must look for the best that is in him.

Bernard Haldane

GOODFINDERS
EXPECT THE BEST
LOYALTY

The *E* in our GEL formula is *Expect the best*. In a seminar a while back I was sharing some of the ideas I've been explaining to you, and a man in the audience came up to me during the break and said, "This information is fantastic. I wish some of those *morons* back at my office could be here!"

My question to you is this: Do you think there is a chance he missed a very important point?

Now let's bring it home to you. What kind of coworkers do you have? What kind of employees? What kind of children? What kind of spouse? So many times we get from others *exactly what we expect*! In short—the way we see them affects the way we treat them, and the way we treat them affects the way they perform.

The Evidence

The feelings and tone that surround us can be changed if we work to change them by sending out the kind of signal we want reflected or echoed. Comedians as well as dramatic performers succeed in creating the kind of mood or atmosphere they want to prevail by sending out the kinds of signals they want mirrored or echoed. "Once you begin laughing," a drama coach explains, "it is easy to continue, for the action and the emotion mutually stimulate each other."

We all have an audience of individuals and colleagues whose day, including their moods, feelings, and dispositions, will be influenced by the way we start it. Hence, sales managers are perhaps the most important "signal generators" for field salespeople, and the expectations of those managers will profoundly affect the performance of the salespeople they lead and supervise.

How Does It Work?

William James, the father of American psychology, concluded that we become how we act. Alfred Adler, another well-known psychologist, later reaffirmed this notion by proving that *if we make ourselves smile, we actually feel like smiling.* In short, our moods match our posture, and more important, people around us tend to feel as we feel. Mood is contagious.

B. F. Skinner, the foremost disciple of the psychological school of behaviorism, contends that our behavior is impacted by the home, school, work, and other environments and that behavior is shaped by consequences. When a sales manager, for example, sends signals to sales personnel that they are regarded as highly competent, effective, capable, and mature and that their work as well as the manager's is meaningful, significant, and worthwhile, the sales personnel who receive those signals will respond in many instances by performing more competently and effectively. And they respond further by perceiving their work as more rewarding, gratifying, and self-fulfilling. The *self-image* is the key to human behavior. Change the self-image and we change the behavior. Even more than this, the self-image sets the boundaries of individual accomplishment. It defines what one can or cannot do. Expand the self-image, and we expand the area of the possible.

Through the power of expectation, a sales manager (or any manager) can develop an adequate, realistic self-image in personnel that will imbue them with new capabilities and new talents and literally turn failures into successes.

1. Positive Feedback

We have already spent a great deal of time and energy on the importance of positive feedback, and I am confident that you are sold on the importance of this vital area. Remember: Be a goodfinder!

2. Regular Learning and Growth Opportunities

Too often in times of tight finances, training programs are the first area cut. This is the exact opposite of what should happen. In times of financial difficulty, training budgets should be sharply increased.

To quote Tom Peters, "The excellent companies view extensive, pragmatic training as necessity, not as boom-time nicety. . . . You gotta trust 'em, and train the livin' daylights out of them." When asked how he justified large amounts of training dollars, Peters replied, "Management from excellent companies would not ask a question like that!"

On a personal note, the Sewell group of companies in Dallas, Texas, is legendary for their service at all of their automobile dealerships. Yet they constantly invest in the training and development of their people to get even better. Needless to say, we are grateful that part of their investment in training has been with Ziglar Inc. Our staff members have bought many automobiles from them over the years and rave about the service they get.

3. Activities and Information That Prove Our Efforts Are Meaningful, Productive, and Appreciated

I usually make every effort to stay away from absolutes such as "never" or "always," but in this case I am going to make an exception. *Never* under *any* circumstances at *any* time downplay the role of a recognition program in your organization, home, church, or any area of interest. In part 2, "The Science of Top Performance," we will get into the specifics of developing a recognition program. However, let me emphasize right here and now that you must never overlook the importance of this vital area.

When we look at activities and information that prove our efforts are meaningful and productive, we look at a very important area for Top Performers. This is the area in which the manager must make one of the most important "sales" ever made. Others must have a concept or a vision—an idea of what the big picture is all about and how they personally fit in and contribute. The great managers regularly paint vivid word pictures showing their people exactly how this is happening now and what is in store in the months ahead.

This is important because one of the greatest problems faced in society today is the problem of *unrealistic expectations*. In business we might set unrealistic goals or expect our progress within the organization to happen much too quickly. In relationships, we may expect others to do certain things for us or act in a certain manner, and if they do not, we are devastated. Now you may be saying, "Wait a second, Ziglar—a minute ago you were saying that if we expected the best, we could get the best . . . and now you are saying that 'unrealistic expectations' are a problem!" Let me finish.

Unfortunately, *there are very few workers today who know when they are successful on the job*. Oh, they have quotas and some guidelines as to what their activities are supposed to be, but how will they know when they are successful?

What about the manager? If we are supposed to give regular feedback to our people, keep them apprised of how they are doing, and paint the big picture for them, how can we determine what information to pass along?

The Performance Value Package

I believe the answer is in the three-step performance value package. Step 1 is *foundational performance*. This is the level of performance the person must achieve to continue to work with the organization (or in the case of children, to avoid punishment). I call it "foundational performance" rather than "minimum standard" because I don't want people even thinking *minimum*, much less working toward a minimum. With foundational performance thinking, not only do people maintain their positions, but they also build a foundation upon which they can build future successes. We will discuss the specific how-tos of each step in the performance value package in "The Science of Top Performance," but for now let's simply say that the foundational performance is determined by mutual agreement of the manager and employee. The employee shares ownership in the ideas and does not feel put upon, and the manager can lead the employee to better understand the big picture during the discussion.

Good news: Rather than having to encourage employees to reach for objectives and standards, you will often have to work to get them to be realistic about their foundational performance.

Step 2 in the performance value package is *successful performance*. The successful performance is the level of performance that may reasonably and realistically be expected by both manager and employee. Again, the manager and employee determine this level of performance by working together and, through discussion, get a reasonable understanding of what each is looking for as far as a successful performance is concerned. Again, let me remind you that the specific how-tos are in the upcoming section, "The Science of Top Performance."

Step 3 in the performance value package is *value performance*. The value performance is the level of performance that may be expected if everything goes according to plan and the employee excels in all areas. This level provides Top Performers with a target. Again, value performance is determined through sharing and discussion. The manager must be sure value performance objectives cause the individual to really stretch.

One of the most difficult but most important things any manager ever has to do is terminate an employee, and to think this will seldom, if ever, happen again is a real boon! If you will combine the value performance package with what I call *due process*, firings will be dramatically reduced.

4. Generate Desirable and Rewarding Consequences for Others (Remember that 75 to 85 percent of behavior is determined by consequences.)

To me, *due process* means "three strikes and you're out." When an employee makes a mistake, we should be really *pleased*! Why? Simply because we learn much more from mistakes than we do from victories. We should do everything we can to congratulate people when they make an error; we should be delighted (well, almost) with ourselves when we make an error. Once we get over this initial euphoria, we need to analyze *why* the mistake was made and *what* we can do to avoid making that mistake again. And everyone must understand that making the same mistake a third time means termination.

The person *repeating* errors is making a value statement about their feelings and their ability level. The statement this person is making is one of two things: (1) "What happens on the job is really not a high priority in my life. My enthusiasm and commitment levels are just not very high." Or (2) "I do not have the ability necessary to handle this position." Our responsibility in helping ourselves and others to become Top Performers is to discover which of these statements is being made and take the appropriate action. In the case of the first statement, the proper action for employee and organization is to help the individual relocate for their own good and for the good of the company. It may be a tough decision, as management consultant Fred Smith said, but the earlier the decision is made, the less the actual waste.

If the second statement is the case, then our responsibility is to help the employee get the training needed to handle the position. If the skill level needed is beyond the capacity of the employee, you don't have an employee problem, you have a *hiring procedures* problem.

You can best help the employee by helping them find a position in which they can use the skills and abilities they already possess—or be trained to more fully develop these skills so they can be successful.

Does That Stuff Really Work?

Let's look at a specific incident where this concept was applied. Jim Savage once spoke to a group of dentists, their spouses, and their entire office staffs, and they taught him this system really does work. According to Jim, they were a delightful group—very professional, very receptive, and anxious to find ideas that would help them become even more successful in their chosen profession. After the program, they were having lunch together and

Jim sat with the dentists at a large, round table and had one of the most interesting luncheon conversations ever.

One dentist said, "I cannot get my receptionist to make 'tension' calls," which are the daily calls to confirm appointments and/or remind people it was time to have their teeth cleaned. Jim "innocently" asked, "Then why is she still working for you?" Obviously, Jim had touched a sore spot, because the dentist responded with a touch of heat, "Well, good employees are not that easy to come by!"

Then Jim asked, "How good an employee is she?" After spending several minutes rationalizing and justifying, the dentist stopped in midsentence and said, "I am being silly. . . . She really is a good employee, but I haven't given her the proper direction." Jim said it was exciting to see the dentist come to the conclusion on his own. By answering questions, this man was able to discover that:

1. He must *establish* and *sell* the concept of the importance of making these calls.
2. He must *train* the people to meet his expectations.
3. He must *inspect* to make sure he gets what he *expects*.

The good dentist went back to his office and called a conference with his office manager and his receptionist. He started the meeting by saying, "It is my goal to pay each of you more money! Would you be interested in discussing how this might happen?" He definitely had their attention! After their enthusiastic nods of approval, he continued, "As both of you know, our office handles 60 to 75 percent of our capacity [based on hours of the day and potential clients] each month. To give you both a substantial raise, we need more clients. One very good way to get additional clients is through appointment confirmation, which will cut down on our cancellations and no-shows. Another way is to make 'business-building' calls. In the past, these have been called 'tension' calls, because the emphasis has been on the one making the call. From now on they are 'business-building' or 'helping' calls, because the emphasis will be on the one we are calling. We have services these people desperately need, and it is our *responsibility* to help them by letting them know when they should be in our office." He went on to say, "Now I know these are demanding calls, and I don't want you to make them all day, so let's start by figuring out how many helping calls it takes to encourage a client to visit our office."

The conversation continued, and by drawing out the ideas of both the office manager and the receptionist (by asking questions), the following resulted:

1. The receptionist would make sure that 100 percent of all appointments were confirmed by starting seven days ahead on calls. She would make calls in the morning, afternoon, and even one call from home each evening, if necessary.

2. The office manager and the receptionist divided the "helping" or "business-building" calls into two equal segments. Five calls each day was foundational performance; eight calls each day was successful performance; ten calls each day was value performance level. A single sheet record report was developed by the office manager that enabled everyone involved to gather and compute the information they needed to see how the program was working. The report was submitted to the dentist weekly.

3. In only sixty days, appointment no-shows were almost entirely eliminated (a side benefit was the excellent public relations created), the office was operating at 85 to 90 percent capacity, and the office manager and receptionist had received substantial raises. Note: The dentist got what he wanted (more clients) because he helped his assistants get what they wanted (a raise). The assistants got what they wanted (the raise) because they helped the clients get what they wanted (healthier, more beautiful teeth and gums).

When we break our goals into bite-size pieces and set foundational performance levels, successful performance levels, and value performance levels, we know *when* we are successful and *how* to get to our Top Performance level. One excellent manager stated: *"If you can't measure it, you can't manage it."*

"I Hate My Job"

One day just before I was scheduled to speak in Birmingham, Alabama, a woman came backstage for a brief visit. She was nicely dressed, but she had completely forgotten to put on a smile before she left home. She walked in and started her little talk—which was apparently well rehearsed. "Oh, Mr. Ziglar, I'm so glad to see you! I hate my job and everybody there, and they treat me terribly." (She was the kind of person who could brighten up a whole room—by leaving it. As the late Cavett Robert would say, "She looked like the cruise director of the *Titanic!*")

She obviously had a lot of experience in dumping a full load of garbage on anyone who would sit still. I got the impression that she expected me to sit there and let her dump all that garbage on me.

I even have an idea that in her mind she expected to leave our interview wiping the corners of her eyes with a little handkerchief, saying, "Oh, you've just helped me so much! I'm so glad you had time to share this with me!" But if I had taken that approach, I would have betrayed everything in which I believe. The *last* thing she needed was sympathy. She needed

> Remember: You find what you look for in life.

empathy instead. She needed someone who was not part of the problem but who could help her find a solution.

When she finally took a breath of air so I could slip in a quick word edgewise, I looked at her and said (firmly but not unkindly), "Yes, your situation doesn't sound very good, and it's probably going to get worse!" If I'd hit her in the face with a bucket of ice water, she could not have been more surprised.

She obviously expected that "nice Mr. Ziglar" to be entirely different. She reacted by jumping back and asking, "What do you mean?" Zig: "It's very simple: Your situation's going to get worse because there is a good chance you may lose this job; and jobs, even bad ones, aren't that easy to find." Woman: "What are you talking about?" Zig: "Ma'am, there's not a company anywhere that can have that much negativism in one concentrated spot and survive."

A few tears started to form, and she asked, "Well, what can I do?" Zig: "I've got an idea, if you're really interested in solving the problem." Woman: "Please tell me what it is, because I'm definitely interested."

Zig: "The first thing I want you to do tonight when you go home is to take a sheet of paper and list everything you like about your job and your company." Woman: "That will be easy, because I don't like anything about it!" Zig: "Now hold the phone and let me ask you a question." Woman: "All right." Zig: "Do they pay you for working there, or do you work there for benevolent reasons?" Woman: "Certainly they pay me for the work I do!" Zig: "Well, the number one thing you like about your job, then, is that they pay you for doing it, so go ahead and write it down. We'll start our list right now."

Look for what you want—not for what you don't want.

Before we finished, we had flushed out twenty-two things she liked about her work: three weeks paid vacation, health and life insurance, five days annual sick leave, all the national holidays, a profit-sharing plan that vested upon retirement, only a ten-minute drive from her home to the office, a full hour for lunch, participation in employee/employer relations, a beautiful building to work in with protected private parking spaces, and so on.

You can take the most outstanding man or woman, husband or wife, boy or girl imaginable, nitpick them to death, and manage to find some fault with them. Or you can take the average man or woman and start looking for the good qualities, and you will find them in abundance. It depends on what you're looking for.

You can take your job or your company and find many good things you like or a number of things you don't like. It depends on what you want out of life because *you are going to find what you are looking for*. Significantly, the more good or bad you find in yourself, your mate, your job, your kids, your country, or your future, the more good or bad there will be to find.

Accentuate the Positive

I encouraged the woman to take her list of twenty-two positive things about her job and, just before she went to bed, get in front of the mirror and enthusiastically say aloud, "I love my job," and add each of the twenty-two listed reasons to the statement. I pointed out that every time she said, "I love my job," she was really saying, "I'm grateful for my job." Gratitude is the healthiest of all human emotions. I assured her that she would sleep better that night. I encouraged her to do this every morning and every night for twenty-one days. During that day and in the days ahead, she was to add more positives to that list.

Expect the best from yourself and others!

That woman left in an entirely different frame of mind. She was no longer a beaten and defeated person. When she walked out, she was actually *striding*. Don't misunderstand. I'm not implying that in a few minutes we were able to overcome a lifetime of her making an overdraft on the bank of right mental attitude. However, we did give her some hope and a plan, and those are two powerful ingredients. As a matter of fact, winning managers never make promises to their people unless they give them a plan to make the promise possible. And when managers make demands on anyone, they extract a plan *from* that person as to how he or she can realistically meet that demand.

Six weeks later I was back in Birmingham doing a follow-up sales training session. The woman was seated right in the front row, grinning so wide she could have eaten a banana sideways.

I chatted with her briefly and asked her how she was doing. She responded, "Wonderful, Mr. Ziglar. You can't believe how much the company and the people who work there have changed!" But of course what had really happened was:

1. She changed because she had enrolled in Automobile University and started listening to my audio series on her way to and from work.
2. This change of input in her mind changed her self-talk.
3. She became a goodfinder—not a faultfinder.

—————— **PERFORMANCE PRINCIPLES** ——————

1. We generally get from others what we expect.

2. The difference between good and excellent companies is training.

3. You find what you look for in life.

4. Never make a promise without a plan.

5. Happiness, joy, and gratitude are universal if we know what to look for.

6

"Wait for Me, I'm Your Leader!"

An ounce of loyalty is worth a pound of cleverness.

Elbert Hubbard

GOODFINDERS

EXPECT THE BEST

LOYALTY

The *L* in our GEL formula stands for *Loyalty*. Loyalty, for managers, is remembering that while you don't work twenty-four hours a day for your company, you do represent your company twenty-four hours a day. If you are going to be a Top Performer, there can be no question about your loyalty in three areas. You must be loyal to yourself, to those with whom you live and work, and to your organization.

Be Loyal to Yourself

To be loyal to yourself, you must work to maintain a healthy self-image. This is not an overinflated ego or the kind of self-confidence that the wit says "generally occurs just before we really understand the situation."

Loyalty to yourself means looking for the evidence that supports *why* you should believe in yourself.

Dr. Laura Schlessinger says the best way to feel good about yourself is to do things you are proud of. Obviously, your self-image will play a major role in how high you go in your company, because it plays a major role in your ability to develop leaders who will follow you on the ladder of success.

This list is not a "brag" list. As a matter of fact, no one should see it but you. This list has nothing to do with conceit. As I often say, "Conceit is a weird disease that makes everyone sick *except* the one who has it!" This list is to help you remember you are a person of worth.

Remember, success is not measured by how you perform compared with how others perform. You may have twice their ability—or half their ability. Success—*real* success—is measured by how you do compared with what you could be doing with the ability God gave you. This means success can also be defined as "not who you are but *Whose* you are."

Yes, a healthy self-image is critically important for Top Performers and managers who wish to become more effective and continue to move up in the game of life. Obviously, I'm not talking about an inflated super-ego, giving the appearance that you are the "greatest of all" but simply a healthy self-respect for your inherent abilities and what you've been able to accomplish thus far in your life. Let's look at some additional steps for improving the way we feel about ourselves.

Step 1: Social philosopher Eric Hoffer said, "In times of change the learners shall inherit the earth, while the learned find themselves beautifully equipped to deal with a world that no longer exists." While Tom Peters, business management author, said, "Only those who constantly retool themselves stand a chance of staying employed in the years ahead."

The good news that goes with this is that when you are growing and learning new things, you feel better about yourself, and that is transferred to the people you are responsible to in your position as a manager and leader. We must clearly understand that we teach what we know but we reproduce what we are.

Step 2: Feeling good about yourself—not arrogant but good—means you will be able to develop people who will have the same feelings about themselves. Their confidence goes up and their productivity along with it.

Businessman Clarence Francis said, "You can buy a man's time, you can buy his physical presence at a given place, you can even buy a measured number of his skilled muscular motions per hour, but you cannot buy enthusiasm. You cannot buy loyalty. You cannot buy devotion of hearts, minds or souls. You must earn these." In the process we will relearn the fact that you don't build businesses, you build people—and when you build your people by being the right kind of leader and setting the right example, your reputation as a Top Performer and a superb manager and person will grow.

Step 3: When you feel confident and comfortable with yourself, you will have an infinitely better chance to make the people that you work with confident and part of the team. Eighteen percent of workers in corporate America do not contribute to the team, and not only do they not contribute, they actually spread poison and create all kinds of problems. When we invite them to join the team and treat them like team members, we dramatically eliminate the possibility that they will become "poison spreaders." The bottom line is that as a manager you will be proud of your people because you will have transformed, productive individuals who become a productive team. You will feel good about yourself because you are making others feel valuable and good about themselves.

Step 4: You also can feel good about yourself if you are taking care of yourself physically, mentally, and spiritually. In 1976, the research of A. H. Ismail of Purdue University revealed that physically fit people are more intellectually inclined, emotionally stable, composed, self-confident, easygoing, and relaxed. It sounds like we've just described a Top Performer, doesn't it? When I started eating sensibly and exercising regularly in 1972, I lost the thirty-seven extra pounds I had been carrying for twenty-four years of my adult life. I've got to confess that I felt better about myself because of my increased energy and, according to the Redhead, I looked better as well. So to feel good about yourself, take care of your body. You'll be glad that you did.

Step 5: One of the best ways to feel good about yourself is to make others feel good about themselves. There is even a great deal of joy that comes along with this, and joy is far more than happiness. Happiness depends on happenings; joy is a spiritual dimension and makes a difference in our lives.

James Howard, president of Honinteg (honesty and integrity) International, says that for performance and profitability you should take the SIR approach. This is an acronym for Short Interval Reporting, which is essential for effective measurement. Mr. Howard points out that many times when our people are assigned responsibilities, they perform superbly. Unfortunately, in 93 percent of the cases, management says absolutely nothing about that good job. He states that the benefit of short interval reporting is that you can give short interval recognition, which is essential for effective motivation. When you can find something good about a performance, whether it occurs once a week or once a month, to compliment the employee about it builds his or her self-image. The individual performs better, which makes you feel better—which again goes back to the fact that you can have everything in life you want if you will just help enough other people get what they want.

Yes, it does take training, and the reality is that our people stay where they grow and are respected and appreciated. With training you add value to the employee; then the employee adds value to the company.

Step 6: You can improve your own self-image and that of your group by encouraging everybody to become a student in "Automobile University"—utilizing the time you spend in the car by listening to audiobooks and podcasts. Years ago Stephen Joe Payne, a Native American from Bartlesville, Oklahoma, entered Automobile University. Today he is fluent in eight foreign languages and translates for his company in Spanish and French. Needless to say, he feels much better about himself, his future is brighter, and he has become more valuable to his company; and he tells me that 90 percent of the time required to learn the languages was used while driving in his automobile—only 10 percent of the time consumed took place elsewhere. His time involvement was minimal, his benefits astronomical.

According to a study from Stanford University, 95 percent of people who buy an idea or a concept are unable to follow through because they do not have the resources to do so. Resources include training, seminars, books, and audio resources. When we help our people to grow (and as a leader/manager that is our responsibility), both their loyalty and performance are significantly higher, and hence they become more valuable to the company. In the process, because you are developing Top Performers, top management sees you differently, and your climb to the top is much faster and far more certain.

Step 7: Guard against time thieves. Make a plan and do what you must to follow through. Avoid idle chatter, because idle chatter means two people are stealing company time. This improvement and increase in productivity saves money—and every dime of that goes to the bottom line. Your value to the company and to yourself goes up. At the end of the day you will have done a job you are proud of.

Be Loyal to Those with Whom You Live and Work

Samuel Gompers, an early labor leader, said the number one objective of any business should be to make a profit, because if it doesn't make a profit, the business fails. Then both employer and employees are out of work, sometimes for a very long time. The best way for a company to make a profit is for management and labor, owner and employee, to think in terms of what each can do to make the company a profitable one. Employees should certainly give it their best effort. Employers should understand that the best way to get their employees on the same page and work with that concept is to treat them with respect and dignity, understanding that they are people with feelings and rights.

Fred Smith spent virtually all of his business life in the corporate world, where he held high positions in significant companies. His office, because he dealt with labor negotiations, was always near the back door of the plant. He explained that this way, as workers were leaving, if they had anything to say—if they had any complaints or simply wanted to talk—they could easily step into his office for a visit. This way he came to know them as people. He knew the names of their spouses and often their children. The bottom line is that, because he knew them and they knew him, in all of his years of work with and through the unions, not once was a strike ever called at the plant where Fred Smith was in charge.

I think it's clear that everyone—management, labor, owner—understands that when a strike occurs, everybody loses. The company loses revenue and labor loses income and profit that is never really regained, so both company and labor end up losing. Strikes can be terribly expensive, and more importantly, when a strike is over, the attitudes and relationships are frequently not the same. There is always a feeling of "We won; they lost," or "They won; we lost." This builds resentment and certainly is not conducive to increased productivity. So the concept of always being on the same side certainly makes sense. Good managers, those tuned in to what is going on, will work to make certain it happens.

As my mama would say, *It's not who's right, it's what's right*, and what I've just laid out is the right approach to growth.

When I think of growth, I think about Sir Edmund Hillary. You will remember that in 1953 Sir Edmund and his native guide, Tenzing, were the first men to climb Mount Everest, the tallest mountain in the world. Hillary failed in several of his early attempts and on one occasion left five associates dead on the side of that great mountain. Parliament wanted to recognize these valiant efforts, so they invited Hillary into their chambers. They even placed a picture of Mount Everest at the front of the room. When Sir Edmund Hillary entered the room, Parliament rose as one to give him a standing ovation. When he saw these legislators standing and applauding his good efforts, tears filled his eyes. Many members of Parliament noticed the tears and must have thought, *Ah, look, the tears of happiness that we are recognizing this good effort he has made.* But they were not tears of happiness and joy—they were tears of anger and frustration! For Edmund Hillary had not set out to make a "good effort" toward reaching his goal, and he certainly had not set out to leave five associates dead on the side of the mountain.

The greatest enemy of excellence is good!

As Hillary walked to the front of that room, he recognized something that many of you have recognized, and that is, yes, he had made a good effort to climb the mountain, but the greatest enemy of excellence is good! Sir Edmund Hillary walked to the front of the room, looked at that picture, and shouted, "You beat me this time, but you are as big as you will ever be . . . and I am still growing!"

You see, my reading friend, if you are in a growth posture—regardless of what you have already accomplished or have not accomplished—there are still great things left in front of you, but you must continue to grow to fully utilize your inherent ability. Remember what Ralph Waldo Emerson said: "What lies behind you and what lies in front of you pales in comparison to what lies inside of you."

When employees move into the management role, they often feel they must know *everything* about their new position. This is an overwhelming burden to carry. They were not hired to be an encyclopedia or a computer— they were hired to manage. Managers don't have to have total recall, but they must know where to find information. Those who can think for themselves are much more important than those who can regurgitate facts. Remember: *It's very difficult to be over-trained!* So get involved in continuing education, seminars, books, and other educational resources. Your thirst for knowledge and understanding must never cease—but you don't need to memorize the manuals for every seminar you attend. Determine that you will continue to grow and learn as a manager, and you will greatly improve your self-image.

> Focus your attention on those you are responsible to and for.

We must never overlook the fact that our company can spend millions and millions of dollars on buildings, computers, electronic gear, fixtures, communication systems, and so forth, but the full utilization of these monumental expenditures is entirely dependent on the growth, training, attitude, and capability of the people in the company. The responsibility for that growth, training, attitude, and capability rests squarely on the shoulders of management.

One of the fastest ways to improve our own self-esteem is to focus our attention on others. Often, the more we think of ourselves, the less self-confidence we have. Forgetting about *us* and becoming sincerely interested in *them* will lead us directly to a healthy self-respect. When you give your full and undivided attention to others and concentrate on making them feel comfortable, you become less self-conscious.

Dr. Alfred Adler said that we can be cured of depression in only fourteen days if every day we will try to think of how we can be helpful to others. David Dunn wrote a wonderful little book entitled *Try Giving Yourself Away*, which gives some marvelous insights as well as some simple, practical steps on *how* we can be an encouragement and help to others. When we are sincerely interested in others, we don't have time to direct negativity toward ourselves.

"Mr. Ziglar, I Heard What You Said"

One Saturday afternoon several years ago, my wife and I were scheduled to play golf at a beautiful course in the Dallas area. On this particular day we had a one o'clock tee time. However, on Saturdays the course attracts many local residents as well as people from other cities, so our tee time was delayed a few minutes. The foursome in front of us consisted of two couples, and one of the young men was on the tee box getting ready to tee off.

As my wife and I sat in our cart, I could not help but notice the young man. He was about thirty years old, something like six feet, three inches tall, and about 220 pounds. However, as the young man stood there addressing the ball, it was obvious to me that he was not a golfer. He looked a little uncomfortable and was addressing the ball in an unorthodox manner. He picked his club up, wiggled it a few times, then put it down and repeated the process for what seemed like an eternity.

Finally, I muttered under my breath that he obviously was not a golfer. My wife quietly asked how I knew, and I responded that I'd been playing the game a long time, had watched a lot of golfers, and just *knew* he was not a golfer. In the meantime, the young man kept wiggling the club and picking it up and putting it down. Finally, he pulled his club back and proceeded to bust that ball about 240 yards, right down the middle. So much for my expertise in evaluating golfers!

After the young man hit the ball, he walked over to his cart, put his club in his bag, and then walked straight back to me. He was neither smiling nor frowning, but as he walked up to me, he said, "Mr. Ziglar, I heard what you said."

Now, my reading friend, I want you to think with me just for a moment. Had you been in my position, what would you have thought—and done? I felt some apprehension and wanted to pull a disappearing act, but fortunately the young man continued: "When you spoke in my hometown three years ago, it completely changed my life. I just want you to know, Mr. Ziglar, it is an honor for me to even be on the same golf course with you."

Needless to say, I breathed a deep sigh of relief, thanked the young man profusely, and was grateful at the sudden unexpected and delightful turn of events. I also made a resolution that day to be far more careful in my judgmental attitude when I am observing or dealing with other people.

I've often thought of how tragic it would have been had the young man actually heard the cutting, unkind, and, as it turned out, untrue remark I made about him. It undoubtedly would have adversely affected him and certainly would have lowered his opinion of me. Not only that, but it would have been virtually impossible for me to have positively affected him in the future from an inspirational and instructional point of view.

As managers and leaders, one of the things we cannot escape is the fact that when people look to us, we have a responsibility to let them see that we deserve to be in that position of leadership. They evaluate and respond to us to a large degree based on the way we see them, feel about them, *and* treat them. That's why it's so important for us to look for the good, expect the best, and always remember that as managers we are role models for many of the people in our group or company. It is at least reasonably important that they like us. It is critically important that they respect us. It is difficult, if not impossible, for them to either like us or respect us if we make snide, judgmental, unkind, and/or untrue observations about them as I did the young golfer.

Don't misunderstand. Each one of us—including that young man—is responsible for our own actions and conduct. By no stretch of the imagination am I responsible for what someone else does. However, I am responsible *to* that person to be fair, honest, objective, and exactly what I appear to be. As a manager in your organization, you are not responsible *for* your people, but you are responsible *to* your people.

HONESTY + COURTESY = LOYALTY

The Forum Corporation of Boston, Massachusetts, did an in-depth study of 341 salespeople from eleven different companies in five different industries. Of this group, 173 were top salespeople and 168 were average salespeople. The primary difference between the two groups was not skill, knowledge, or ability. The 173 super salespeople were more productive because their customers *trusted* them, and customers are far more likely to *believe* the honest salesperson. They discovered that people do not buy based on what you tell them *or* what you show them. But they *do* buy based on what you tell them *and* show them, which they believe. The same principle applies in directing the activities of those under your leadership. They will "buy" and act enthusiastically on your leadership based *only* on what you tell *and* show them. Anything less than that trust and confidence simply means they will give less than their 100 percent support.

In managing people, trust and honesty are commodities we can take to the marketplace and cash in at any time. Top Performers in management learn to create trust in others by *complete* honesty in all dealings.

The second characteristic these super-successful salespeople possessed in spades, according to the *Forum Report*, was plain, old-fashioned courtesy. These salespeople were just as nice and courteous to the receptionist and file clerk as they were to the office manager and accountant. They were as pleasant with the shipping clerk and service personnel as they were with the president of the company. The reason is simple: They clearly understood that the sales process is not complete—and future sales are in jeopardy—until the current sales order has been delivered, installed, serviced, and paid for and the customer is satisfied. For this reason they *knew* they needed the cooperation, effort, and goodwill of the entire team back at the home office.

In any business or family where two or more people are involved, there is always going to be a certain amount of discussion and conflict about who does what. One of the best opportunities for teaching trust and honesty is in the area of responsibility or doing what needs to be done. Unfortunately, in most businesses and homes the battle cry is, "That's not my job!" Top Performers, however, are loyal to those with whom they work and live and show this loyalty by doing what they are supposed to do, when they are supposed to do it. They give strong verbal support and never say negative or unkind things about their associates. They clearly understand that when you're slinging mud, you're not doing anything but losing ground. Top Performers also are willing to go the extra mile and do the extras, because they instinctively know that the more successful their company or department is, the more likely they are to move ahead in their own careers.

Burke Marketing Research asked executives in one hundred of the na-tion's one thousand largest companies, "What employee behavior disturbs you the most?" The result was "a hit parade of things that stick in the boss's craw, the kind of behavior that hits a nerve," said Marc Silbert, whose temporary personnel agency commissioned the survey. "They can blind employers to employees' good qualities. They become beyond redemption," he said. Liars, goof-offs, egomaniacs, laggards, rebels, whiners, airheads, and sloths—these are eight banes of a boss's existence, according to the survey, with *liars* topping the list. "If a company believes that an employee lacks integrity, all positive qualities—ranging from skill and experience to productivity and intelligence—become meaningless," said Silbert. Obvi-ously, loyalty to those with whom we live and work is a prerequisite to Top Performance.

Be Loyal to Your Organization

When I say that loyalty to your organization is important, I do not mean you should accept every thought that comes from upper management as if it had come down from the mountain on tablets. No one expects you to leap with joy when the commission structure has been changed so that there is more for the company and less for you. You are not expected to thank ownership when the working hours are changed and you are allowed to work more hours for the same or less pay. Loyalty to your organization means handling these aggravations in the proper manner.

Let's take a "negative break" and talk about how *not* to handle these situations. You do not complain about your areas of concern over coffee with a coworker who has no authority to change the situation. You do not identify internal problems externally—meaning to someone outside your organization. The person who takes either of these avenues becomes a cancer to the organization. As you know, a cancer is a cell that lives within the body independently of the other cells of the body, and unless it is removed, it will eventually lead to the death of the body. There are few diseases that will affect your organization in a deadlier manner or will creep up on the company with less notice than lack of loyalty. I have already mentioned that I feel very strongly about the importance of due process, but if there were ever a reason for dismissal without due process, it would be a lack of loyalty.

How, then, should the loyal employee manage the situation? The proper method of handling any situation that concerns you is to take the *problem identified* to someone who has the authority to handle the situation. Present it and several *potential solutions* for consideration. If after a realistic amount of time, the company takes action on your recommendations or provides another satisfactory solution, you should congratulate yourself for working from within the organization to make it stronger.

However, if after a realistic amount of time, the company fails to take action to change the situation, you now have two options: (1) shut up, or (2) move on. There are no other options! If you continue to identify a problem over which no action is going to be taken, then the cancer grows and you are beating your head against the proverbial brick wall. I believe that ulcers, serious headaches, burnout, stress, and even heart problems often begin in this manner. Dr. David Schwartz, in his book *The Magic of Thinking Big*, says that over 80 percent of our hospital beds are filled with people with "EII," or Emotionally Induced Illness. This does not mean that the people are not sick, just that their illnesses *began* in their minds.

You owe it to *yourself*—as well as to your organization—to either support what is happening or find another company to work for. Now some of you are saying that good jobs are not that easy to come by, and I agree. Neither is the human body that easy to come by—at least, spare parts are in great demand! The answer is simple but not easy: Get with the program or find another program to get with!

A Final Word on Loyalty

We began this chapter with a quote from Elbert Hubbard, and now let's close with some wise words from the same man:

> If you work for a man, in heaven's name *work* for him. If he pays you wages that supply you your bread and butter, work for him—speak well of him, think well of him, stand by him and stand by the institution he represents. . . . If put to the pinch, an ounce of loyalty is worth a pound of cleverness. If

you must vilify, condemn, and eternally disparage, why, resign your position, and when you are outside, damn to your heart's content. But, I pray you, so long as you are part of an institution, do not condemn it. . . . [If you do that] you are loosening the tendrils that hold you to the institution, and at the first high wind that comes along, you will be uprooted and blown away . . . and probably you will never know the reason why.

Krish Dhanam's grouping of the following words sums up the message:

Plan with attitude,

Prepare with aptitude,

Participate with servitude,

Receive with gratitude,

and this should be enough to

Separate you from the multitudes.

PERFORMANCE PRINCIPLES

1. Loyalty begins with loyalty to self.
2. You cannot consistently perform in a manner that is inconsistent with the way you see yourself.
3. Make every effort to be perceived as the most capable, not the most visible.
4. The greatest enemy of excellence is good.
5. If you don't have something nice to say, don't say anything at all.
6. Support your organization or go to work for an organization you can support.

7

On Great Leadership

David Mattson

Servant leadership is all about making the goals clear and then rolling your sleeves up and doing whatever it takes to help people win. In that situation, they don't work for you; you work for them.

Ken Blanchard

Given the choice of any topic that I wanted to cover in this book, I didn't hesitate. I knew instantly the question I wanted to address, a question that Zig Ziglar himself often addressed: *What makes a Top Performing leader?*

In following Zig's insights (and his personal example), I'd like to suggest that it's the exact opposite of the stereotypical "Type A" cartoon executive who barks orders, demands instant obedience, humiliates subordinates, and constantly threatens to fire people (whether or not he follows through on those threats). That's not really leadership, as anyone who's ever accomplished an important, complex objective by leading a team can attest.

The greatest leaders adopt a very different model, a model that has come to be known as *servant leadership*.

Servant leaders, who in my experience are the most successful leaders, don't focus on the world according to me. They don't get fixated on the organizational chart. The organizational chart may say, "You work for me," but servant leaders tend to take a very different approach. Their attitude with direct reports (and others) is: "You don't work for me—I work for you."

If you have that kind of relationship with your direct reports, what you find is that the relationship doesn't need the hierarchical structure of the organizational chart in order to benefit both sides. The working relationship isn't positional. It doesn't have anything to do with what is printed on your business card. It is relationship based. And it works because the leader in question says and *means* things like: "I am interested in what you are doing." "I care about what is going on in your world." "I am personally invested in helping you figure out how to do your job better so that you become more successful in what you are doing."

Notice that is me helping you—a very different dynamic than me making sure you do what I want.

If we aspire to be great leaders, that means we want to be interested in our people. And by the way, since the organizational chart does exist, it's always a very positive thing for the recipient when someone higher up in the organization displays the kind of authentic interest that I'm talking about! It usually makes a huge difference in employee attitude when someone up high shows genuine interest in somebody at a level below them. As a leader, you can use that to your advantage. But here's the catch: You have to mean it.

Learn to Show Authentic Interest

Servant leaders make time to explore what's happening *outside* the workplace, not just how the latest project is going. They take the time to ask appropriate questions about what is going on in the daily lives of their direct reports. How is the family? What's going well? What kinds of bumps in the road are people experiencing? What's the next big life milestone on the horizon? These kinds of questions, when asked with genuine interest, can create powerful *relational* connections with your direct reports that have nothing to do with who reports to whom. Do what too many leaders fail to do: Ask. Ask about parents. Ask about kids. Ask about educational plans. Ask about any obstacles (professional or otherwise) that the person has run into. Find out what's going on right now in their world. And *listen* to what comes back.

Most leaders we work with ask their direct reports questions and then move on mentally to the next topic before the answer is given in full. Or they seem to pay attention, but their nonverbal signals send the clear message to the employee that they are being "polite" by not talking but really don't care about what's being said. *Listening is more than waiting for your turn to speak.* It is a conscious decision to be "you-focused" rather than "me-focused" and to respond appropriately and empathetically to what you hear. You have two ears and one mouth. As a leader, consider the possibility that you should use them in roughly that proportion. Don't dominate conversations. *Steer* the conversation based on interested questions, and let the other person do the talking—much as you would during an effective sales call.

A good test of whether you are being an active listener is to ask yourself whether you can recite the details of what has just been said to you. After a conversation with a direct report, if you can only rattle off a few main points (or can't remember anything at all), you need to work on your listening skills. Active listeners can recall not just the details of what the person just said but his or her emotional state and level of comfort while communicating. Servant leaders are usually very active listeners, which means they can recall the nuances of the exchange—specifically, the places where the person was comfortable and the places where he or she was uncomfortable.

Servant leaders also tend to know and understand the *communication strategies* of their direct reports. This only makes sense. If we are interested in them as people, then by default we have to understand what their communication style is, and we have to play to that. If you don't know what your own dominant DISC style is, and what each of your direct reports' dominant DISC styles are, you owe it to yourself and to them to find out.[1]

Servant leaders learn to *spot and examine the most relevant information in the exchange.* This is a key point. I may not like what you're saying, or the way you're saying it, but I still have to listen to you because there may be something important in what you've shared that I need to take into account. It's my job as the leader to figure out what that something is. I have to listen to what is being said, I must not be distracted by how it is said or who is saying it, and I have to watch out for my own bias.

If I start thinking, "Here comes Jim—he's always such a complainer," I may miss out on an important opportunity to listen for the truth that Jim may have to share with me. Even if Jim *is* complaining about something, he may have information I can't get from any other source or a unique perspective that I need in order to solve an important business problem. So I want to listen attentively to him with full respect. If I discount Jim before he even starts to speak, I do a disservice to the relationship, and I do myself a disservice as a leader.

Real Leaders Align Personal Goals with Company Goals

The most effective leaders know that people work harder for their families and themselves than they will ever work for the company. Great leaders don't *just* articulate and reinforce a compelling vision. They realize that's part of their job, of course, but they don't stop there. They connect the dots. They look at what will motivate specific individuals to help them make that vision a reality.

This means making a shift from thinking only about what motivates *us* to thinking about what motivates *others*. Motivation to support the company mission may be second nature for us, but it is at least one step away from what really matters most to most working people. They are more likely to be motivated by the prospect of protecting and nurturing the people they love, or attaining important personal goals (like getting married), or securing the kind of leisure time they feel they deserve.

We need to recognize that service to the company mission is removed from those kinds of goals—the goals that really motivate employees. It's our responsibility as leaders to connect the dots.

What sometimes makes this difficult is that we've connected the dots so well in our own lives that we assume that everyone else—and specifically our direct reports—must have done more or less the same thing. The reality we may lose sight of is that: they usually haven't. When we focus on the company and we think that's good enough because we pay them, we're missing an important step.

Here's an interesting exercise I have asked leaders from just about every industry to do. I say: "Take a moment now to write down your two biggest 'why' factors—the reasons you get up in the morning to do what it is you do all day long. *Why* are you doing all the sacrificing? *Why* are you working so hard? What are you hoping to accomplish with all that work?"

The CEOs, owners, and senior executives I'm talking to will all write down their reasons. Then I'll invite people to share what they came up with. Invariably, what I hear are personal reasons, not business reasons. (For instance: "I want to keep my family safe, well provided for, and happy.") I'll point out that the executives in the room have *already* connected the dots between those personal goals and their professional ambitions. That's why they work so hard!

Then I'll say, "Let's pretend we just had a great year and, as a result of that great year, you got a check for $250,000. That was your bonus this year. Tell me the three things you would automatically do with that money. What's on the dream list for you?"

They write down their responses. Then we go over a few of the entries, which tend to support the *why* factors we already identified. (For instance: "Take my family on a vacation trip they'll never forget and buy my daughter a nice car.")

Then I say, "Okay—what if I were to tell you that we have a 70 percent chance of hitting that target this year so that you can earn that bonus . . . but in order to make that a 100 percent chance, you would have to stretch a little in two or three areas. Would you be motivated to do that?"

The answer is always Yes! The executives tell me they would be highly motivated to go above and beyond the call to earn that $250,000 bonus at the end of the year.

And then I say, "Guess what? That process I just did with you is exactly what you need to do with team members who report to you!"

How many of us have even taken the time to sit down and talk with the people who are our direct reports to find out what the most important personal goals on their horizon are? That's what great leaders do. They have that discussion. They make it tangible. They help their people connect the dots. They say, "Okay, what happens if you do get the promotion? What happens if you do get the bonus? What would you do with that money?" Then they find ways to help people align with those unique personal goals, *visualize* them on a daily basis, and make sure their behavior supports the attainment of those goals.

That's what we really have to do if we want to be great leaders for our organization. We have to show a genuine interest in our own people; we have to help them connect the dots between what they're doing for themselves and what they're doing for the company; and we have to make sure their progress along that road is something that truly matters to them on a personal level. If we can build effective working relationships with the right people, relationships that are based on these principles, then the possibilities really are limitless—and we're in a much better position to follow through on Zig Ziglar's famous promise: "See you at the top!"

PERFORMANCE PRINCIPLES

1. Leaders work for their employees.
2. Servant leadership is relational.
3. Great leaders understand communication styles.
4. Real leaders align personal goals with company goals.

8

"People Just Don't Care...."

One learns people through the heart, not the eyes or the intellect.

Mark Twain

Unfortunately, as managers of people we often feel like the speaker who was met with less than a resounding welcome and said, "In the words of Willie J. Shakespeare, it's nice to be among friends . . . even if they are somebody else's." So many times managers and their employees almost seem to work at developing an adversarial relationship. Instead, we have to be like the small boy who was confronted by three big bullies, any one of whom could have obliterated him. (They even gave some indication they were going to do exactly that.) Like a lot of us, the little guy wasn't too well qualified to fight, but like *all* successful managers, he was qualified to think. (In this case, his physical well-being depended on it!) With this in mind, the little guy backed up dramatically, drew a line in the dirt with the toe of his shoe, looked the leader of the group in the eye, and said, "Now you just step across that line." Well, as you might imagine, the big bully confidently—even arrogantly—stepped across the line. The small boy then smiled broadly and exclaimed, "Now we're both on the same side!" If we are going to be successful in managing people, we have got to remember that managers and the people they manage *are* on the same side.

As I mentioned earlier, Sir Edmund Hillary and his native guide, Tenzing, were the first people to make the historic climb of Mount Everest in 1953. Coming down from the mountain peak, Sir Edmund suddenly lost his footing. Tenzing held the line taut and kept them both from falling by digging his ax into the ice. Later Tenzing refused any special credit for saving Sir Edmund Hillary's life; he considered it a routine part of the job. As he put it, "Mountain climbers always help each other." Can we, as managers, afford to be any different? Aren't we obligated to work with our people to direct their energies and help them to develop their skills and talents to the fullest?

Your Billion-Dollar Asset

It is my firm conviction that if you can take only one thought or one idea out of *Top Performance*, it should be the thought I will share with you now. If you would really like to be an expert in the "people business" (that determines 85 percent of your success), then you should look into this statement: People don't care how much you know until they know how much you care . . . about them!

Chances are great you have heard that phrase before, and as an achiever, you really don't need to be told—but it doesn't hurt to be reminded. You see, whether we are talking about parents, brothers and sisters, children, spouses, friends, associates, coworkers, employees, or employers—people don't care whether you are a Phi Beta Kappa from MIT or if you got your PhD from Harvard. They don't care if you have twenty years of experience (or one year of experience repeated twenty times), sold more units for more dollar volume than anyone else ever has, or set every record the company keeps *until* they know how much you care about them.

Anyone can do a job; anyone can do a *good* job. But it's not until there is love in a person's heart for a job that the results are something that others will call *great*! Love is caring—caring enough to invest your life, to give it your all, to stick it out, to do the best you possibly can.

Love comes forth to contribute, to invest, to help, to be a loyal part of an effort or enterprise. Love will draw out from a person the very best they can do, which is often more than that person or anyone else thought they could do. Love motivates one's entire potential for that individual's total success. But love also serves to inspire others to motivate the ones who follow them.

Now, serving and giving part of ourselves is not a popular practice in society today, but think with me for just a second. When you come in at the end of the day and your spouse greets you at the door, chattering like a magpie about something in which you are totally disinterested and you stop and give him or her your undivided attention, aren't you giving your loved one a part of your life? Aren't you giving up a little of yourself?

> People don't care how much you know until they know how much you care . . . about them!

When you have been dealing with people—not always successfully—all day, what you really want is a few minutes of peace and quiet in front of the evening news or with the newspaper. Just as you settle down, your children, whom you dearly love but want to love from a distance for the next few minutes, come climbing on you as if you were a jungle gym. At this point, when you either turn off the TV or put the newspaper down so that you can give them your love and undivided attention, you are investing a part of your life in theirs and giving up part of yourself. When you are dead tired because it's been "one of those days," and an employee needs an empathetic ear and counseling, and you take the time to listen, aren't you giving up some of yourself?

If you want to be an expert in the people business, read the Performance Principle at the end of this chapter, brand the words on your heart, and live them every day of your life.

PERFORMANCE PRINCIPLES

1. People don't care how much you know until they know how much you care . . . about them.

9

The Five *P*'s
of a Top Performing Business

Howard Partridge

Either you run the day, or the day runs you.

Jim Rohn

If you own a small business, do you remember *why* you went into business for yourself? Was it to make a lot of money? Or was it because you were tired of being managed and you wanted to be your own boss, to chart your own course—to have a little more free time?

The brutal reality of most small business owners' lives is that you *are* the manager at the helm! You feel like a slave to the business; there's very little free time; the business consumes your mind 24/7; there's major stress, no *real* freedom, and your day is consumed putting out "brush fires."

Can you relate to that?

I sure can.

I started my first business out of the trunk of my car over thirty-four years ago, and I made good money, but I worked twenty-four hours a day, seven days a week. I was a slave to my business. I loved to travel, but much of my supposed "vacations" were spent on the phone talking to clients and employees back home.

Then in 1997, I began to learn the secrets of a Top Performing business and transformed my first company into a predictable, profitable, multimillion-dollar business that's turnkey. Today I have phenomenal systems and a phenomenal team in place who love their jobs. As a result, I don't have to be there. But what's more important is that for over twenty years, I've helped thousands of small business owners around the world do the same.

In 2008, I invited Zig Ziglar to speak at one of my conferences. Tom Ziglar was impressed with what he saw, and we began our business relationship. Since 2011, my training company, Phenomenal Products, has been the exclusive small business coaching company for Ziglar. Since then, Tom and I have traveled the world helping small business owners stop being a slave to their business and transform it into a predictable, profitable, turnkey operation.

Currently, we have coaching clients in over one hundred industries in nine countries. Every day we get incredible testimonials from business owners who are making more money personally, growing their businesses by leaps and bounds, and most importantly, spending more time with their families. After all, no amount of business success can compensate for failure at home.

You *can* build a Top Performing business that will make a predictable profit, that also gives you the freedom you've always wanted . . . if you know how to manage yourself well.

The Five *P*'s of a Top Performing Business

Secret #1: Purpose

A strong purpose is the *why* behind your business. A powerful purpose energizes everyone involved. Zig Ziglar said, "Man was built for purpose. He was designed for accomplishment, engineered for success, and endowed with the seeds of greatness."

The greatest business lesson I ever learned, and the greatest business lesson I believe you can ever learn as a business owner, is that your business exists for one reason and one reason only: to be a vehicle to achieve your *life goals*.

Zig said we must become a meaningful specific rather than a wandering generality. He created a phenomenal tool to help you develop a vision for your life. It's called the *Wheel of Life*. You can use it to assess where you are on each of the seven spokes of life and to set goals in each of those areas.[1]

And of course, part of your life goal is to make a difference in the lives of others, right? Not only is it important for you to be clear on *why* you do what you do but a strong *purpose* is vital to engaging your team.

Your life goals are not just about you.

Discovering the *why* behind your business gives you energy to do the difficult tasks of running your business, and it engages team members to understand how their work makes a difference in the lives of others. Renowned author Jim Collins of *Good to Great* fame says, "Meaningful work means a meaningful life."[2]

Finally, a powerful *purpose* connects with your prospects and clients in a very special way. In his viral TEDx video and bestselling book *Start with Why*, Simon Sinek shares that most companies are *what* companies—they make widgets. Some companies are *how* companies—they have a different spin on the widget that differentiates them from the competition. But the greatest companies are *why* companies, because they *make a difference* in the lives of those they serve.

To create a *purpose* statement for your business, think about what your team and community would be missing if your business didn't exist.[3]

Secret #2: People

Zig taught, "You don't build a business, you build people, and people build the business." I've found this to be true. If you hire the wrong person, it doesn't matter what else you do; nothing will work. All of business and all of life is about relationships. A Top Performing manager understands that everything is about people.

Building people starts with building yourself. If you haven't developed yourself as a leader, it will affect the performance of your entire team. Everything rises and falls on leadership, and the toughest person to lead is yourself! It starts with you. You have to *be* before you can *do*, and you have to *do* before you can *have*. If you want to *have* a Top Performing business, you must *be*come the business owner and leader you need to be.

In order to *be*come the leader you need to be, you need a coach. The *right* coach. You'll be hard-pressed to find a Top Performer in any discipline who got there without the right coach. Not only do Top Performers have a coach but they have a coaching *team*. Think about the greatest athletes. They have specialists in every area. If I had to pick one thing that helped me in my business more than anything else, I would have to say it was having the right coach in each area of my business.

Zig Ziglar's career was launched with a kick in the pants from a man named P. C. Merrell. At that time, Zig Ziglar wasn't exactly a "top performer." In fact, he was struggling. During a training event, Mr. Merrell, a highly respected sales trainer at the company Zig worked for, took him aside and said, "Zig, I've never seen such a waste! If you learned how to believe in yourself and started work at the same time every day, I believe you could be a great one." And a great one he did become.

Gary Keller, cofounder of Keller-Williams Realty, the largest residential real estate company in America, reports that the company's meteoric rise began with working with a coach. He writes in his book *The ONE Thing: The Surprisingly Simple Truth Behind Extraordinary Results*, "Accountable people achieve results others only dream of. . . . One of the fastest ways to bring accountability to your life is to find an accountability partner. Accountability can come from a mentor, a peer or, in its highest form, a coach." Keller also cites the research of psychologist K. Anders Ericsson on expert performance that revealed "the single most important difference between amateurs and elite performers is that future elite performers seek out teachers and coaches and engage in supervised training, whereas the amateurs rarely engage in similar types of practice."

As a business coach myself, I can tell you that I've seen the results in our coaching clients. They are making more money, having more fun doing it, and experiencing less stress, and they have more time with their families.

Our most successful coaching clients just do two things: They learn the proven systems, and they implement them. Simple as that.

Learning is the easier part. Implementation is the harder part. In fact, the number one reason small businesses don't grow or do as well as they could is what I call *F.T.I.* (Failure To Implement). Good coaching solves that problem. But just one coach can be limiting, so I've assembled a team of experts and a community of fellow business owners who support one another, encourage one another, and help one another be accountable to their biggest dreams and goals.

In order to perform at the highest level, we need access to those who have already traveled the road. And they need to be experienced in knowing how to help others get to where they are going. During the California Gold Rush of the 1800s, a man by the name of Lansford W. Hastings sold a guide to immigrants that would supposedly make the trip much faster. The problem was that he had only traveled the route twice and had never led a wagon train on that route. The Donner Party suffered the consequences. Half of their party died in one of the most tragic tales of that time.

Top Performance requires a top coaching team,[4] and it also requires a strong team within the company.

You need a strong team to reach your dream of having a Top Performing business. If you have a dream but no team, you have to give up the dream or build up the team. In order for you to have a Top Performing team, your team members must be trained in the technical areas of their work and in soft skills such as building winning relationships, personality styles, and leadership.

When team members know how to better communicate with one another, they will get better results, have more fun doing it, experience less stress, and make fewer mistakes. Seventy percent of American workers are disengaged because they don't think leadership cares about them. Zig Ziglar said, "No one cares how much you know until they know how much you care *about them.*" If you really want to take it over the top, help them reach their personal goals, encourage them, and help them become better people. This is a seemingly magical combination that creates incredible loyalty.

You may feel that training is expensive. After all, what if you invest in training an employee and they leave your company? I love how Mr. Ziglar answered this question: "The only thing worse than training an employee and losing them is not training them and keeping them!"

For five decades, leadership studies have found the exact same thing. Performers leave companies for other reasons—not pay. By the way, be aware that Top Performers won't stay at a company that isn't a Top Performing business. They won't stand for mediocrity.[5]

Secret #3: Plan

A Top Performing business doesn't just happen. Zig said you were born to win, but in order to be the winner you were born to be, you must *plan* to win and *prepare* to win before you can expect to win. When you plan to win and prepare to win, you can *expect* to win.

Success doesn't happen by accident. Many business owners get distracted and tend to spend their day reacting to circumstances rather than creating a vision and a road map. One of my favorite quotes is: "Vision without action is just a daydream. Action without vision is a nightmare." To be a Top Performer, we need a game plan!

This is one of the reasons a coach is so vital. A good coach helps you focus on where you really want to go and helps you get there. Your team members are key to creating the plan too. A leader shouldn't plan the business all alone. In fact, when you get your team involved in the *plan*, they will help you make it happen. They take ownership.

Think about one year from now. How do you want your business to be different? What would your business need to look like to give you the results and the freedom you really want? How much profit would it have to produce? Would you need more staff? What's working in your business now? What isn't working? What steps do you need to take to get to your goal?[6]

Secret #4: Processes

If you want better results, more freedom, and less stress, your business will need systems. A *predictable, profitable* business requires a *process*. A *process* takes the pressure off the person.

Remember that your business is a *vehicle* to help you achieve your life goals. When you jump in your automobile, you assume the combustion system will fire off to ensure the car will be able to run. If there isn't any gas in the vehicle, it won't run. And if the engine isn't operating properly, it doesn't matter how much gas the vehicle has, you'll have problems on your journey. If the electrical system isn't working properly, your instrument panel won't work, and you won't have any feedback on how you are progressing. How much gas do you have? How long before you arrive at your destination? What is your speed?

Finally, if the driver doesn't know how to drive or doesn't know where he or she is going, you have a real problem! You're not really going anywhere; you're just taking a drive. That may be okay if that is your goal, but my guess is that there's a destination in mind! By the way, what I just described are the five systems every business needs to have.[7]

Secret #5: Profit

My experience has been that when you learn *and* apply the previous four secrets, your company will become phenomenally profitable. And that's important, because you want to pay yourself for the work you do in the business as well as make a healthy profit for the risk of owning the business. Plus, you need cash to absorb unexpected situations and to take advantage of new opportunities.

A business without a profit is just a hobby. And a twenty-four-hours-a-day, seven-days-a-week job is not a very exciting hobby! Profits don't happen by accident. In fact, without diligently watching your numbers, it's really easy to let profits slip.

I've experienced that too. Many years ago, I got my companies in a lot of debt. Life became about making the monthly payments on a maxed-out line of credit and high-interest credit cards. Something had to change.

I *purposed* to get out of debt and hired a financial consultant by the name of Ellen Rohr (*people*), who gave me a *plan* and a *process* to make a *profit* every single month. I got debt-free personally, and our companies are debt-free except for equipment purchases, which help us leverage the balance between tax deductions and operating new equipment rather than the cost of old equipment.

Today, through our business coaching and training, we've helped many others handle unexpected expenses, cover potential cash flow issues, and take advantage of any opportunities that may arise. This takes time and diligence, but it may not take as long as you think.

If you self-manage your own business, I know you will be encouraged by the many amazing stories of small business owners just like you who have more money in their accounts than ever, have built a phenomenal team, and have systematized their businesses (and of course have more free time as a result) that can be found at www.ZiglarTraining.com/smallbusiness.

PERFORMANCE PRINCIPLES

1. Know why your business exists.
2. Build your people and they will build the business.
3. Proper planning creates a road map to success.
4. A process makes your business more predictable.
5. A business without a profit is just a hobby.

PART 2

THE SCIENCE OF
TOP
Performance

Science is organized knowledge.
Herbert Spencer

10

"But I Thought You Said ..."

> Precision of communication is important, more important than ever, in our era of hair-trigger balances, when a false or misunderstood word may create as much disaster as a sudden thoughtless act.
>
> James Thurber

Every manager has heard about the importance of *communication*. Yet we all need to be reminded occasionally just how important it is, and we need some specific suggestions on what we can do to be more effective. We also need to remember that miscommunication, poor communication, or no communication can create incredible problems.

In this chapter we will examine some of the problem areas that inhibit communication, review some of the rules for better communication, and take a closer look at specific situations, such as public speaking and meetings, in order to maximize effective communication. Finally, we'll see how communication plays a part in creating a work environment that is conducive to productivity.

According to the *Harvard Business Review*, the most promotable quality an executive, manager, salesperson, or anyone can possess is the ability to communicate. Alan Loy McGinnis, in his excellent book *Bringing Out the Best in People*, tells why:

> Motivators always use words lavishly and intensely as they outline their dreams to prospective supporters. Such diverse leaders as Lyndon Johnson, Winston Churchill, and Lee Iacocca have all possessed something in common: a mesmerizing ability to talk. Some may have had their shy sides, but when the occasion presented itself, each could pour out a profusion of words. "The inspiring talker produces zeal," said Aldous Huxley, "whose intensity depends not on the rationality of what is said or the goodness of the cause that is being advocated, but solely on the propagandist's skill in using words in an exciting way." Words are a remarkably powerful vehicle. Much of Franklin D. Roosevelt's success was due to his ability to coin a phrase and use slogans to summarize his dreams, and those slogans became a part of the fabric of our national life. Gandhi and Martin Luther King, Jr., both knew that if one speaks long enough, there is an uplifting and elevating, almost intoxicating power in words. Most of us have experienced it hundreds of times—listening to another speak, either before an audience or in one-on-one conversation, until the sound of their words and the sheer weight of their flow eventually persuades us.
>
> You can gain a considerable following if you are willing to relate your message to enough people and not be deterred by those who don't buy it. Instead, you pick up your idea and present it to the next prospect. Eventually, with enough presentations to enough people, a few people become enthusiastic, they join the parade, one by one, and soon a movement is on its way. Talk may be cheap, but the right use of words can generate in your followers a commodity impossible to buy . . . hearts on fire!

In the corporate world, miscommunication can have a disastrous effect on productivity. Any time you think, *They probably know*, let that be a red flag to remind yourself that they probably *don't* know—and seize the opportunity to *remind* them of what they should know.

According to AT&T, the lion's share of time spent in any office is spent communicating: listening, talking, chasing down stray facts, dealing with mail, etc. Were you to keep a log, you'd be appalled at how little time you have for actually producing work (par for senior executives is about 15 percent of the workday).

In addition, communication can be very difficult, and it takes a constant, concise effort to make sure you are understood. Communication should be as crisp and to the point as the sign I saw on a newly restored home when I was in Chattanooga. It read, "Trespassers Will Be Shot—Survivors Will Be Shot Again." To be effective communicators, we should always be just that clear, though not necessarily that threatening.

As Easy as EBP

The problems in communication in the management area, and in society for that matter, are so great that we at Ziglar have developed a seminar for companies and individuals called Presentation Skills Training, which has enabled men and women from all walks of life to dramatically improve their communication skills. Our corporate staff spends two days coaching and recording their presentations. The participants are amazed and delighted at the remarkable difference in their first presentation and the one at the end of the second day.

Seeing yourself as others see (and hear) you is important, so participants are videotaped a dozen times, given private coaching sessions, and instructed in twelve vital skill areas. Effective Business Presentations is an extremely strong skill builder because approximately 30 percent of the time is spent on instruction, while 70 percent of the time is spent on practicing skills each individual needs and can use *immediately* upon returning to the job. Now this is beginning to sound a little bit like a commercial because it is—a commercial for gaining communication skills! Let me give you a sample of some communication skills and ideas from our seminar that you can use immediately.

Did You Know That . . . ?

You have about four minutes to be either received or rejected when you first meet someone. You gather 87 percent of your total lifetime information by sight; 7 percent by hearing; 3.5 percent by smell; 1.5 percent by touch; 1 percent by taste. So when you encounter a prospect or an employee, what they *see* is vitally important. Listeners need visual stimulation—a point of activity to focus on. Gestures, body language, and facial animation, in addition to other visual stimuli, are crucial. The average person *speaks* at about 150 words per minute but *thinks* at about 600 words per minute—or about four times faster. You may think your mind wanders, but in fact it often is *galloping* ahead of you like a runaway racehorse. As a communicator you must do everything possible to hold the listeners' attention, including keeping your thoughts in order and paced with your speaking.

The Dazzling Dozen

You can become a more effective communicator by becoming aware of what we call the twelve *vital skill areas* of communication. These areas are appearance, posture, gestures, eye contact, facial expressions, voice, padding, involvement, handling of questions, humor, introducing others, and visual aids.

Appearance means your clothes plus the way you groom, the way you carry yourself, and your accessories. Your appearance makes a statement about you; it tells others what you think of yourself. What does *your* appearance say? Does it add to or detract from the message you wish to communicate?

Posture means body language. Does your body language say that you are confident and in control, that you really care about the person you are communicating with, and that you are comfortable—or does it communicate just the opposite?

Gestures are the specifics of body language as it relates to arm and hand movement. You have heard people say they couldn't communicate if they couldn't use their hands, and that is at least partially true. Natural arm and hand movement allows communicators to express themselves much more clearly.

Eye contact is to the eyes what the handshake is to the hands. When we "clasp" eyes with someone, we send either positive signals of confidence, courage, interest, and concern or negative signals of boredom, irritation, disgust, antagonism, or even anger.

Facial expressions include the smile and frown. Your face is one of your greatest assets for effective communication. With controlled facial expressions, you set the tone for conversations and let people know what's coming. You also show what you mean and make your thoughts easier to follow.

Voice includes not only the pitch of your voice but also volume, inflection, and pace. When you vary the volume level, place emphasis on certain words and phrases, and speak at a varying pace, you become more effective and are far more likely to be understood.

Padding is the nonworking words that we so, uh, often, um, insert, ah, into, you know, our—well, like, our, uh, um, ah, spoken conversation. Just for fun, record a telephone conversation (your side of the call only) and count the number of nonworking words. You may be surprised.

Involvement means active listening, both on your part and on the part of those who might listen to you. Using a person's name, asking questions and listening to the answers, and speaking in terms of others' interests are examples of how we involve others in communication.

Handling of questions is especially important in business conversations. All too often we do not listen to the question or do not answer the same question that is asked. If integrity and trust are important in business (and they are), then the way you handle questions can increase your trust level with those with whom you work.

Humor can be used to relax your audience (of one or ten thousand) and make friends with them. It can also be used as a bridge when you are shifting into other, perhaps more serious, subject matter and as a way of giving your audience a mental break. It can be especially effective in lengthy presentations to bring a tired or drifting audience back to the session. Careful—don't overdo it. Too many would-be communicators sacrifice message for humor. Incidentally, the rule for sharing questionable humor of an off-color nature is this: If you have to ask the question, "Should I share this?" you already have the answer: *No!* (I've never known a speaker to get a speaking engagement, an employee to get a promotion, a salesperson to make a sale, or a politician to win votes because he or she used profane language or told off-color stories. However, I do know of countless instances when extremely negative reactions were the result of profane language, tasteless stories, or sexist or racist comments.)

Introducing others may not seem very important to you, but someone very wise said, "You never get a second chance to make a first impression." In introductions, you have the opportunity not only to make an excellent first impression but also to make others feel important through sincere recognition of their strengths.

Visual aids are not only used in board meetings but may also be used in one-on-one conversations. Any time you can impact more than one of your listener's senses, you are ahead in the communication game.

By just being aware of these vital skill areas, you will move ahead in communication skills. And if you spend time working and studying in these areas, you can substantially increase your communication skills.

Differences between Oral and Written Language

Even though you may be an excellent writer, you will not be an excellent oral communicator if you use the same approach in speaking as you do for the written word.

- Spoken language must be easily and instantly understandable to listeners. If the listeners misunderstand, they cannot go back and reread.
- Spoken language should be more repetitive. It is important to re-phrase several times the key ideas you want the listeners to take away with them.
- Spoken language should be simpler in structure than written language.
- Figurative language adds life and color to spoken words. Colorful, descriptive words can turn an otherwise colorless phrase into a memorable one. Lincoln described a nation "conceived in liberty." Kennedy spoke of freedom as a "torch passed to a new generation." CBS wordsmith Charles Osgood said, "Compared to the spoken word, a picture is a pitiful thing indeed."

PERFORMANCE PRINCIPLES

1. Miscommunication, poor communication, or no communication will create problems.
2. Get involved in communication training that teaches both sides of the communication process—speaking and listening.

11

Recognizing, Rewarding, and Role Modeling for Top Performance

The greatest humiliation in life is to work hard on something from which you expect great appreciation, and then fail to get it.

Edgar Watson Howe

Bringing out the best in people means appreciating what they do, rewarding them for it, and giving them the role models they need to become Top Performers. In this chapter we'll take a look at these three important aspects of successful management.

Recognition

Several years ago I was scheduled to speak at a banquet in Dallas for an insurance company. During the meal I was seated at the head table between two company vice presidents. We were chatting amiably as the meal was being served. When our waitress placed a salad in front of me, I said, "Thank you." A few minutes later when the bread was placed in front of us, I again said, "Thank you." When she brought the entrée, I not only said, "Thank you," but added, "You know, I want to tell you how much I appreciate the good service you're giving us. It's amazing how you work so efficiently and yet don't seem to be in any kind of hurry. More important, you're so pleasant and gracious, and I just want you to know I appreciate your efforts." She beamed broadly, thanked me for my comments, and said I had made her day.

While all of this was going on, the two vice presidents on either side of me were ignoring her or acknowledging her service with a grunt. They directed all of their comments and attention to me and our conversation. Dessert time was quite an eye-opener. When the scoop of ice cream with chocolate syrup was delivered, the two vice presidents received a scoop about the size of a golf ball. I received one about the size of a baseball. The difference was so obvious that both of them simultaneously commented, "Well, Zig, I see you know this lady." I laughingly said, "No, I've never met her before tonight, but I do know a lot about her." They asked how I knew. I pointed out that she was a human being and, like everybody else, she wanted appreciation and sincere interest, and I had given her both of those things.

The same thing is true of every member of your organization and family. Everyone likes to be appreciated. What better way to express your appreciation than to share a simple, courteous "thank you" when something pleasant has been said or some simple service has been rendered. Obviously, I was not being nice to the waitress in the hope that I'd get a bigger scoop of ice cream. To be honest, I didn't need the bigger scoop—I needed the smaller one. But because I fed her needs, she responded in the only way she could—which was to dig deeper and get a bigger scoop of that ice cream. I believe that in helping others to become Top Performers by teaching them to be thoughtful, kind, and considerate of the other person, we are teaching them to dig deeper and get a bigger scoop out of life.

Not a "Pollyanna" Philosophy

Art Pollasky, regional manager for Snap-on Tools in Crystal Lake, Illinois, has learned how to dig deeper and get a bigger scoop. He says that people are motivated by money and a deep-rooted desire to do something significant with their assigned roles and responsibilities. As a young sales-man selling office forms with the Burroughs Corporation, he bought into the philosophy that you can have everything you want in life if you will just help enough other people get what they want. The result was the beginning of a successful and stellar sales career that took him all the way to the top. While visiting with him on a project some years ago, I had the privilege of getting to know him better. I can say that this young man, who wore out his first set of training tapes as he searched for new and improved ways to garner an edge in his professional career, is today reaping the rewards of all that effort. The greatest joy comes in hearing what those around him say about his integrity and his passion. Both Bryan Flanagan and Krish Dhanam have worked very closely with Art and constantly extol the style and flexibility with which he conducts his sales profession and his life.

In 1982 the *Wall Street Journal* carried the following article by Jack Falvey entitled, "To Raise Productivity, Try Saying Thank You." I believe you will benefit from these concepts.

> Managers often think of themselves as systems specialists or problem solv-ers or functional experts. They lose sight of the commonsense practicality of getting others committed to doing things for them willingly. The essence of good management is letting people know what you expect, inspecting what is done, and supporting those things that are done well. The experts acknowledge that we don't know the design limitations of a human being. All we do know is that even the most committed people seldom exceed 15% or 20% of their brain capacity in a normal day's work. Average people can double or triple their output with increased confidence, more encourage-ment, better organization, a deeper commitment, and a surprisingly small amount of effort. Additionally, if managers would begin thinking in terms of doing things for their people—instead of to them—we would see pro-ductivity increases off the scales. . . .
>
> Here are a few things you can do right now with no increase in budget, but with big returns.
>
> Set up informal visits with your people. Listen and use your eyes to pick up on what is going on. Don't look for problems, look for strengths and things done well. Make something out of every positive thing you can find. As a manager, your words and actions carry impact much greater than you

expect. Just a small effort with these techniques will have an almost immediate effect. A concentrated, disciplined, and sustained thrust in these directions will produce incredible returns. Publish everything positive you can find. Print is cheap. Its rewards are long lasting.

Put positive notes on solid productive efforts and send them back to the producers. . . .

How innovative can you be? Do you realize the impact you have on others? Can you reduce or eliminate the negatives in your dealings with your people? Will you do the searching and analysis necessary to uncover positive contributions? Can you name the strengths of your people? Can you, do you, say something complimentary to your Top Performers on a regular basis?

As simple and as straightforward as all this is, it is really a tremendously difficult professional challenge. Just how good are you as a professional manager? *If results are produced by committed people, just how much time and interest can you spread around to build that commitment and get those results? Go do something nice for someone or say something nice to someone right now.*

Recognizing Top Performance

Most managers would like to have employees and coworkers who take *pride* in their careers. Now since *pride* means many things to many people, let's look at a workable definition for our purposes.

To me, PRIDE is Personal Responsibility In Daily Effort. If we are going to encourage those around us to take personal responsibility in daily effort, we must recognize the importance of *recognition* in this process.

The late Mary Kay Ash, founder of Mary Kay Cosmetics, is generally credited with having said that *everyone* carries a sign that is constantly on display: Make Me Feel Important! If we can do this (make others feel important)—*sincerely*—then we have taken a giant stride in developing Top Performers.

Everyone needs recognition. The blue-collar worker is recognized for being the family provider; the white-collar worker is recognized for having great potential; the sales/marketing person is recognized for having high-income–earning power. The point is that some people's recognition needs are very basic, while the needs of others may be quite complex. The Top Performers in the world are *builders*, *doers*, and *competitors*, and they

121

want to, and even need to, make a contribution to whatever they do. They must know when they are contributing and how much they are contributing. Those who manage Top Performers develop a "scoring" system that keeps everyone informed of how they are doing. Please remember that negative scoring should be done in private and positive scoring should be done publicly.

Developing Enthusiastic Optimism

To develop Top Performers, we must teach them how to be enthusiastic about life, how to graciously deal with other people, and how to encourage others. When you develop a pleasing personality by being a little friendlier and more outgoing, it can be enormously helpful to you socially, professionally, and, for that matter, spiritually. Let me share an incident with you that demonstrates some important concepts.

I never realized just how tough working on a cafeteria line could be until my youngest daughter, at age sixteen, tried to find a job—and the only one she could find was on a cafeteria line. As I watched what she had to do and contend with, from both customers and management, I promised myself I would never again go down a cafeteria line without saying something pleasant, gracious, optimistic, and enthusiastic to every person on the serving line. And I still do this today.

One particularly hot August day after the lunch hour crowd had departed, a friend of mine and I were going down the cafeteria line and I was "doing my thing." The gentleman in front of me was apparently from the same school of thought, and he, too, was giving pleasant greetings and encouragement. This worked quite well until he got to the meat department and made the mistake of saying something about the day. The woman serving the meat put her hands on her hips, then wiped her forehead with her right hand and literally slung the perspiration to the floor as she proclaimed, "Yes, this is one of *those* days!"

Now I'd like to point out that she was not talking to me, but when you understand the business I'm in and the reputation I have as a positive thinker, combined with the fact that I had an associate with me, you must understand that my reputation was at stake. So, though it definitely was none of my business, I proceeded to stick my big nose in and say, "Yes, today is absolutely beautiful, isn't it?" With that she looked at me with disgust and said, "You have been out in the sun too long!" I replied, "No, actually I've just come back from overseas—and I've seen grown men and women without anything to eat, small children without any clothes to wear, sanitary conditions that are impossible to describe, and poverty beyond your wildest imagination. And I look at you today. You're young, pretty, employed, and an American citizen. I know for a fact that you could take this job and do it to the best of your ability, and someday you could well be the manager of this place. For that matter, if you really bought into the American dream with all its possibilities, you could eventually own a place of your own."

Personally, I thought it was a superb, impromptu, off-the-cuff speech, and I was reasonably confident she wanted to express her appreciation for my willingness to share with her those words of hope and encouragement. However, for fear she might miss her lead-in, I decided I'd better assist her a little, so I paused and said, "Now you feel lots better, don't you?" This time she looked at me with even more disgust and said, "You—are—sick!"

Stinkin' Thinkin' at Its Worst

As we'd say down home, you win some, you lose some, and some get rained out! This woman was hard-core negative. Her stinkin' thinkin' had gone into an advanced case of hardening of the attitudes that gave every indication of being terminal. I meekly walked on down the serving line, getting the rest of my food and picking up my ticket. My buddy and I sat down to have our lunch and after a few minutes ran out of tea. A petite woman who was at least sixty—and she could well have been seventy—came by serving refills. I don't recall ever seeing anyone her age with as much of a twinkle in her eyes, so I smiled pleasantly and asked my famous question: "How ya' doin'?" She literally took a half step, half jump, half dance backward, grinned broadly, and said, "Honey, if I was any better, I'd think the deck was stacked!" I laughed and said to her, "Well, why don't you go tell the servers on the serving line what you just told me?" In mock horror she threw up her hands and said, "Oh no! I don't want to have anything to do with those girls! If I fool around with them much, I'll end up being just like they are!"

I don't know where that woman learned her psychology, but she was right on the button. The way I read my Bible, it teaches, "Be not deceived—evil communications corrupt good manners" (1 Cor. 15:33 KJV). It's an established fact that your associates do have a strong bearing on your feelings, attitudes, moral values, and conduct. The classic example I often use is this: You can take a Southern boy and send him up North or out West and, after a period of time, he will end up with an accent. Or you can take a Northern or Western boy and send him into the South, and pretty soon we'll have him talking normally! (Yes, I expect you Northerners and Westerners to turn this example around.) We need to be careful whom we associate with, because we do become part of what we are around.

Chances are about four thousand to one that if you were given the choice of being with or around either the woman on the serving line cutting the beef or the older woman serving the tea, you would, without hesitation, choose to be around the woman serving the tea. This book is written so that you can help others be Top Performers, and you do so by helping them become more like the lady serving the tea. You affect this important dimension of the Top Performer's life by recognizing outstanding performance.

Recognition and Rewards Motivate Employees

Years ago, we determined that our company needed a formal recognition program. Since outstanding programs recognize the qualities that are pertinent to company and individual employee success and "sell" them, we began by deciding what qualities we wanted to foster. Based on our needs and beliefs, we determined it was important that our employees came to work regularly with a good attitude and demonstrated leadership qualities that showed they are "part owners" in the company. Top Performers must realize that while the boss may sign their checks, the employee determines the amount.

Our basic needs—attendance, attitude, leadership, and loyalty—evolved into four recognition awards that we distributed quarterly. Here is the information we presented in our employee manual:

The Ziglar Training Systems Recognition Program is based on the premise that "what gets recognized and rewarded is clearly what the company values." Our philosophy challenges each team member to look for the good in others. The Ziglar Training Systems Recognition Program allows us to find that good and recognize exceptional performance. The award categories are fun and usually personalized to the individual receiving the award. Some of the award categories are The Top Performance Club (sales professionals being rewarded for excellence in sales, service, and innovation), tenure awards (different monetary denominations to signify years of service to the company), and special merit (recognition for going above and beyond the call of duty and living the philosophy and mission). In addition, daily and weekly contests involve the sales department and sometimes all the support staff to create a buzz and generate excitement.

What Happens without Recognition?

According to pollster Daniel Yankelovich, who was quoted in *Psychology Today* magazine, workers keeping on-the-job diaries over a ten-year period reported that they had been working with 10 percent less effort than when they initially started those jobs. That's enough of a change to account for the *entire* drop in national productivity over that ten-year time span. But before we start blaming workers, he cautions, his own surveys have shown that the "work ethic" is stronger than ever—workers want to work hard and do a good job. He explains the paradox with the results of another survey showing that workers don't believe that they themselves benefit from increasing productivity. Because they think greater productivity benefits only management, consumers, and shareholders, workers have no incentive to be more productive. The answer, says Yankelovich, is to *directly reward workers for their productivity gains.*

Rewards

Usually when we think of rewarding people, we think of money. *Incentive motivation* is a much-debated form of motivation and for many organizations a viable alternative, especially in the sales field. One of the important things to remember about incentive motivation is, "Today's fringe benefits are tomorrow's expectations." This means that in incentive motivation we must constantly be willing (and able) to "sweeten the pot" to come up with truly motivational incentives.

But the Good News Is: It Doesn't Have to Be Real Money

One summer, Charlie Pfluger from Indianapolis, Indiana, attended one of our Born to Win Seminars for Educators. He really got motivated about the positive approach to education and what could be done with the right attitude under almost any circumstances. Charlie was particularly enthused because he was the principal of an inner-city school that was just one year away from closing its doors. He went back home with a tremendous amount of enthusiasm and, with the wholehearted support of his staff, devised a game plan for the coming year.

Charlie took a silver dollar and used it for the outline of a neat little project. On one side he wrote I CAN and on the other side he put PLA MONEY. As you can see from the diagram below, we've fancied it up a bit.

Charlie's original version was cut from a sheet of paper and was fairly crude but enormously effective. He reproduced them by the hundreds and gave each teacher a supply. When a youngster was "caught" doing something good, such as picking up paper in the schoolyard, cleaning the blackboard without being ordered to, welcoming new students to the school, returning "lost and found" articles, and a host of other things, the student was given an I CAN by the teacher.

When a student received one hundred of these I CANs, he or she was awarded an I CAN T-shirt. Out of a student body of 594, 587 of them won an I CAN T-shirt. It truly became a status symbol. Charlie smilingly says it got to be slightly ridiculous to see a sheet of paper blowing across the schoolyard with five kids out there running it down!

Some of the students helped elderly people across the street, and when a new student showed up, he or she was individually greeted by about ninety-seven students. In short, the entire school got involved in the project.

There are some who may contend that 587 T-shirts was expensive, and, of course, they are right. However, when you consider the results, it's got to rate as the finest investment the school ever made. First of all, there was not a single case of vandalism for the entire year. There was not a single drug bust for the year. Attendance for the year was measurably better; grades were better (in many cases, substantially so); and perhaps best of all, for the first time parents, teachers, and students felt they all were on the same team seeking the same objective.

Role Models

The primary role of leadership is to create a team headed by someone the team can follow because they respect his or her integrity and leadership abilities. Our example from the educational world achieved that objective. The principle will work just as effectively in the business world, as you can see from the following article:

What characterizes a role model? What rings a tone of excellence that is loud and clear? What separates the role model from the rest? Let's look at one.

Nicola Iacocca immigrated to the United States from Southern Italy in 1902 and eventually settled in Allentown, Pennsylvania, where he built a small auto rental business. His son, Lee, surrounded by cars all his life, aspired to work for Ford. With a Bachelor's degree from Lehigh and a Master's from Princeton, Lee joined Ford Motor Company in 1946. By 1970, only the grandson of Henry Ford held a higher position in the company than Iacocca. On July 13, 1978, thwarted by Ford's obsession with nepotism, Iacocca was fired. On October 30, 1978, Lee Iacocca was named president of the Chrysler Corporation; on that same day, Chrysler announced its largest-ever quarterly loss.

On Thursday, April 21, 1983, the New Chrysler Corporation triumphantly announced it earned $172.1 million in the first quarter, the highest quarterly profit in the automaker's history. Initially, many dismissed Iacocca as a hypersalesman. After all, the demise of Chrysler was imminent. Wall Street laughed, the public taunted, Congress scrutinized, and *Iacocca persevered*. After effectively cutting the size of the company in half, Iacocca went to work on the people at Chrysler.

His managerial style has been described as charming, demanding, arrogant, ruthless, and confident. The truth is that *Lee Iacocca demands no more than he gives*. He is the ideal role model. He set quarterly goals for Chrysler, for himself, and for his management team. Iacocca exudes confidence. He is impeccably tailored and groomed . . . and literally oozes assuredness. He is a winner.

Three A's for Excellence

There is, indeed, a common thread of excellence that weaves its way through people like Lee Iacocca. Not surprisingly, although these men and women are involved in completely unrelated businesses, there is a remarkable degree of common factors among them. These common factors, these ingredients for success, represent our three A's for excellence: *Attitude*, *Aggressiveness*, and *Appearance*.

Attitude. Excellence is a mind-set; you must believe. Each person who achieves success seems to have an unwavering commitment and belief in his or her own abilities. They adhere to a very basic tenet of business: Rely on no one. Their beliefs, their mind-sets, and their attitudes are communicable. This is a top-to-bottom phenomenon in organizations. We all want to believe. But when the CEO believes and that belief is transmitted throughout the organization, the belief is catching. During Iacocca's reign at Chrysler, St. Louis plant manager John Burkhart said: "All of us at Chrysler believe in the man."

Aggressiveness. Our society today is overcome with a national lethargy that has reached epidemic proportions. In a multinational, hypercompetitive business environment, we can no longer afford this luxury. The global business community is populated by competitors who are both hungry and aggressive. Perhaps we, too, are hungry, simply not hungry enough. The search for excellence is a top-to-bottom aggressive process. It is a preemptive strike on the business community. First you win, second you lose.

Appearance. A brilliant student could not find a job. He mailed résumés to dozens of businesses. Many responded favorably, inviting the student to visit and interview for a position. The student visited a number of firms, but no offers were forthcoming. The student wanted to know why.

"Are you absolutely certain you want to know why?" his professor asked. "I am," replied the student. The professor then responded, "You look like you've been on a six-month camping trip." The student indignantly responded, "Are you referring to my hair and my beard?" The professor answered, "Yes, and your clothes and your shoes, and your breath." The student said, "That's not fair." And the professor patiently replied, "*You didn't ask if it was fair, you simply asked why.*"

Fair or not, the business community responds to appearance. Naturally, appearance must be fortified with substance but, nevertheless, appearance is important. *You must reek of excellence.* Many of the initial high marks received by the Reagan administration were based not on substance but simply on appearance; the White House once again appeared "presidential." Reagan and his staff looked the part. The sartorial splendor of Iacocca is not an act. The third *A* is simply a visual manifestation of attitude and aggressiveness.[1]

PERFORMANCE PRINCIPLES

1. Everyone needs recognition.
2. Pride = Personal Responsibility In Daily Effort.
3. Outstanding recognition programs recognize the qualities that are pertinent to company and individual success and reward these qualities.
4. The three *A*'s for excellence are:
   a. Attitude
   b. Aggressiveness
   c. Appearance

12

Getting to Know You ... and Me Too!

The primary skill of a manager consists of knowing how to make assignments and picking the right people to carry out those assignments.

Lee Iacocca

Have you ever wondered why you hit it off so well with one person and never could seem to get along with another? Why is it that your new boss seems to be so much more difficult to deal with than the last one? What is it that really accounts for the difference in personality types and styles? People who find the key to unlock these questions have a definite advantage in understanding themselves and others.

What does this have to do with Top Performance? Quite a bit. Top Performers know themselves and know how to deal effectively with different personality types. We don't treat everyone the same. The manager who says, "I treat my people all the same" is going to be very ineffective. If you can recognize some of the basics of different personality types, you will be surprised at the difference it will make in your ability to deal with people.

There is a great deal of information on the market today that gives us insight into the personality types of others and ourselves. Psychologists administer the Myers-Briggs Type Indicator. Dr. Carl Jung, the Swiss psychoanalyst, wrote in *Psychological Types* in the 1920s, "What really accounts for personality differences is that every individual develops a primacy in major behavioral functions." He went on to elaborate on the inherited and developed traits we all possess. At Ziglar we use the Personal Profile System from Performax Systems International. The more we know about ourselves and others, the better suited we are to deal with people in our complex society. Early in my career I would not have considered using a personality profile in hiring employees, and today I cannot imagine hiring anyone without this tool—not just for our sake but for the sake of the employee as well. Let me give you two specific examples.

When Ron Ezinga was considering my offer to become president of the Zig Ziglar Corporation some years ago, we agreed that it would be wise for us to be tested for compatibility. Neither of us was interested in getting involved in a business relationship that was anything less than a workable one, because joining our firm meant Ron would have to resign the presidency of a larger company and move his family over a thousand miles to Dallas. It also meant major changes in our company and a substantial change of direction for me personally. Our getting together seemed natural because I was speaking over a hundred times a year and was substantially less than effective in running our business. Ron's job was financially rewarding but did not permit him full use of his creative skills, organizational abilities, and management expertise. We wanted to get together, but we wanted it to be "right" for our families and our careers.

As prudent decision-making businessmen, Ron and I went through extensive testing and found that we really had the potential for an excellent business partnership. My style is to be quick to act and make decisions, while Ron's is to be very deliberate and gather the facts. The psychologists said, "Zig, if you can speed Ron up a little, and he can slow you down a little, you guys are gonna be really successful!" There were many areas where it seemed his strengths compensated for my weaknesses and my strengths compensated for his weaknesses. The scientific tools validated what we both suspected and prayed would be the answer—that we could successfully work together. And I can tell you that I am so grateful God led Ron to our company at that time. Under his effective and imaginative direction, we moved into many new areas and reached five to ten times as many people as we were reaching before Ron joined our team.

The second example I would like to share pertains to a young woman we hired as a backup receptionist. She was very pleasant and quite good on the phone; however, she was never in her seat when it came time for her to "back up" on the phones. She had so much energy that "sit ability" came hard for her. We had reached the point that we were considering asking her to find other employment when we got involved in the Personality Profile System. From the analysis we saw that *she* wasn't the problem—*we* were! We had completely misplaced her. Fortunately, we had an opening at the time for an assistant office manager. The job required that about fourteen different projects be handled at one time (ordering office supplies, getting office machines repaired, hosting visitors to our offices, etc.), and she was magnificent! She was one of the best we have ever had in the position. We all shed a tear when her husband's career called for them to relocate.

The point is this: With scientific validation we can get reinforcement for making career decisions—both in hiring and in choosing a profession. Am I recommending that your organization get involved with one of these personality profile analyses? The answer is yes. We also have a consulting team that specializes in developing personalized personnel programs for your organization.

A Voyage in "Self" and "Other" Discovery

A personality analysis is somewhat like the analysis of the notes on a musical score. This analysis will reveal the nature, even the quality, of the performance. Every musical instrument and every human being is different. Take any group of people who interact together in pursuit of some common goal and you will see that each person possesses personality traits different from the others. Each of these people is motivated differently, and the differences can result in effective performance (as with Ron Ezinga and me) or in complete discord. This does not necessarily mean that one person is right and the other is wrong—just that we are different. And that's good! If we always agree, then one of us isn't necessary.

The beauty of the personality analysis (regardless of the system used) is that not only does it enable you to understand why you and those around you behave as you do, but it also enables you to take advantage of this knowledge (not take advantage of the people) so that you can channel energies and focus talents in existing relationships for the better. Understanding personality differences helps people appreciate each other more and, consequently, work together more effectively. This, coupled with specific insights into the communication dos and don'ts, creates a real win-win scenario.

Here's how it works: Most of the studies we have done categorize behavioral style into four broad dimensions. Obviously, no one individual's personality can be defined as belonging totally to one of these four categories. We are, after all, human beings and not computerized mechanisms. Our personalities reflect many subtle differences of tone and texture, and we all have some of all degrees of each of the characteristics. However, some characteristics are dominant and will surface on a regular basis.

As you read this information, it is particularly important that you remember the philosophy that you can have everything in life you want if you will just help enough other people get what they want. As you identify these people, you will learn what turns them on, what inspires and encourages them, and how you can help them to become more effective in what they do. All of us are different. This will help you to deal with the different personalities in the people you will be interacting with as a manager and as a Top Performer.

Think of four beakers of liquid that you might find in a chemistry laboratory. Each beaker represents one of four personality characteristics: *aggression*, *people*, *patience*, and *quality*.

How Aggressive Are Your Employees?

The first beaker is our *aggression* container. People whose aggression containers are filled below the midline usually are willing to let others make decisions and are glad to reach decisions by consensus. These individuals are often quiet and unassuming, are perceived as being mild-mannered in dealing with others, and are usually modest about personal achievements.

To motivate these people, place them in low-pressure situations and allow them to lead with a "let's do it together" style instead of a demanding style. Incentive motivation will do little to motivate these good-natured individuals who are turned off by pressure. They are willing and unselfish, which is one reason they are sometimes taken advantage of by more aggressive people.

People whose aggression containers are filled above the midline are often perceived as strong-willed, task-oriented "doers." They have a tendency to drive themselves and others and enjoy change and challenge. You recognize these people by their steely-eyed (stern and intense) expression and clenched fists that pound the table for emphasis (or pointed finger for the same effect). They stride rather than walk, and they always seem to be going somewhere with a purpose and in a hurry.

You motivate these people by challenging them and granting authority. The less tied down they are, the more effective they become. Give them direct answers and stick to business when in the business environment. When you disagree with them, take issue with the facts and not the person. The more you refer to objectives and results and provide facts about success probability, the more you have their attention.

These people will be turned off if you continually demand documentation or require them to follow policies and procedures. They are pioneers, not followers. If you question their authority or place a ceiling on their earning potential and advancement possibilities, they will go to work for someone else.

One of the key concepts to remember when looking at personality characteristics is that our weaknesses are often extensions of our strengths. These individuals are goal achievers who are forceful, decisive, confident, and persistent. They strive to achieve. This may lead to impatience, workaholism, lack of attention to detail, abrasive interaction with coworkers, and overstepping of privileges.

Who Are the "People" People?

The next container is our *people* container. If the container is filled below the midline, it usually indicates people who are unwilling to spend time with other people. Others may perceive them as aloof and pessimistic. These people are usually slow to speak out and at times are suspicious of the motives of others. They are usually very conscientious about the way they handle themselves in the social and work environment and are careful about their appearance.

You motivate these people by providing a work environment free from social contacts. Allow these individuals to think out a problem by themselves. They are at their best on projects requiring logical analysis. Superficial and loud people really turn them off. These congenial though rather reserved people can be quite the problem solvers, but if placed in a position of solving "people" problems, they will be quite uncomfortable.

People who have their people containers filled above the midline are normally very spontaneous. They are enthusiastic, friendly, and good at persuading others to join them. They are perceived as being poised, charming, emotional, and optimistic. You will recognize them by their ready smile and relaxed and friendly manner. They are very expressive with arms and hands and, if you are around them for any extended period of time, they will hug you or pat you on the back, shoulder, or hand.

To motivate these people, give them time to socialize and talk. Let them express their opinions and ideas, especially those regarding people. Help them by being supportive of them in relationships.

These people are turned off by work with long periods of intense concentration, record keeping, and criticism of their friends. Put them in a nonparticipative environment (computer terminal, accounting tasks) and you won't be able to keep them for long. These "people" people are trusting, sociable, generous, popular promoters. But if you go too far in extending these strengths, it may result in more concern with popularity than results, overselling, problem avoidance, and heart-over-mind decisions.

A Measure of Patience

The next container is our *patience* container. If the container is below the midline, these people are usually actively involved and prefer an unstructured environment. They are frustrated by the status quo and invite change. Impulsive, ready to move about, and good at initiation, they are excitable and anxious to get the job done.

You motivate these individuals by giving them a variety of activities and the freedom to move about on the job. The nervous energy they bring to the workforce can be very positive when channeled; however, if left undirected, anxiety, nervousness, and tension will result. The strength of these people lies in the initiative they are willing to take. This becomes a weakness when they initiate so many projects that none are completed.

People who have their patience containers filled above the midline are very stable and have "sit ability." They are recognized for being kind, patient, quiet, disciplined, and service oriented. You recognize these people by their willingness to listen to others and by their friendly countenances. They appear to be relaxed; body movement is smooth and effortless. To motivate these people, give them time to adjust, few changes, and *no* surprises. If you show sincere appreciation for tasks completed, these folks will be extremely loyal to you. Create a secure environment and allow them to develop work patterns for maximum productivity.

These people will be turned off by pressure placed upon them. New tasks and new people presented on a regular basis will produce diminished productivity. These people are loyal, deliberate, sincere, hardworking, consistent, and dependable. They are team players. Their strengths become weaknesses when they procrastinate or are asked to initiate projects. They may have trouble meeting deadlines. They always finish the project—they just like to do it on their own time schedule.

Quality, Not Quantity

The last container is our *quality* container. If the quality container is below the midline, people may be perceived by others as being strong willed (that's a nice way of saying stubborn). People who are low in this container are normally very independent and couldn't care less about details. Quantity wins out over quality with these folks.

You motivate these people by letting them do a job their own way and granting autonomy. They are persistent and will stick to a chosen course of action. This strength becomes a weakness when they stick to a project that would be better off given up.

The people who have their quality container filled above the midline are known for conscientiousness and concern for detail. They are intuitive and sensitive to the environment. These cautious individuals insist on competence and accuracy. You recognize them as thinkers who are seeking facts. They are not highly animated in gestures and are uncomfortable with those who easily show emotions.

To motivate these people, give them personal attention, exact job descriptions, and a controlled work environment. If you allow them to be part of a group or team and provide solid, tangible evidence for your position in discussions, you can win a friend. They are turned off by those who demand quick decisions on important matters and don't allow them enough time to check for accuracy. If you place them in an unstructured environment where no performance guidelines exist, they will find somewhere else to work.

These quality-conscious people are normally mature, accurate, logical, precise folks with high standards. If they take their strengths to the lengths that they become weaknesses, they may overanalyze and get "paralysis of analysis" and become inflexible and bound by procedures and methods. They may have a tendency to get bogged down in details and hesitate to act without precedent.

How Are You Doing?

I hope that as we've been looking at each of these containers you've been doing a little self-evaluation. On a scale of 1 to 10, with 1 being very little and 10 being ready to overflow, how would you rate your *aggression*, *people*, *patience*, and *quality* containers on the chart below? How would your peers rate you? How would you be rated by your employees, and so on down the list? Let me remind you of something I said earlier: We all have some of each of these qualities. There are times when our containers seem almost empty and other times when they are almost full. However, I think you can see that each of us has dominant characteristics.

Aggression	People	Patience	Quality
I say___	I say___	I say___	I say___
Parents___	Parents___	Parents___	Parents___
Employees___	Employees___	Employees___	Employees___
Spouse___	Spouse___	Spouse___	Spouse___
Children___	Children___	Children___	Children___
Boss___	Boss___	Boss___	Boss___

If we take each of these containers and line them up next to one another, we can get a comparison of how we stand in each area. Remember that the farther away from the midline, the stronger the characteristics are perceived by others.

	Aggression	People	Patience	Quality
10	Direct	Enthusiastic	Predictable	Perfectionist
9	Daring	Persuasive	Relaxed	Accurate
8	Risk Taking	Emotional	Nondemonstrative	Systematic
7	Decisive	Trusting	Deliberate	Conscientious
6	Competitive	Sociable	Stable	High Standards
			Midline	
5	Calculated Risk Taking	Reflective	Outgoing	Opinionated
4	Self-critical	Factual	Eager	Persistent
3	Weighs +/-	Controlled	Fidgety	Independent
2	Peaceful	Self-conscious	Restless	Rigid
1	Quiet	Suspicious	Active	Firm

Some of you (those in the upper half of the quality container and lower half of the people container) have noticed the overlapping characteristics. These feed each other. In other words, people rating themselves a 3 in people and an 8 in quality have the ability to analyze and should excel in positions allowing them to use their strengths. To place one of these people in a public relations role may not be advisable for long-term consideration. It is not that they could not perform in this position. The question is, For how long and at what cost could they do that job?

The beauty of these tools when they are applied in a scientific manner is that for hiring purposes you get the round pegs in the round holes and the square pegs in the square holes. When they are used after people are already in position, they allow you to help the employee take advantage of their strengths by working in a position they not only enjoy but in which they can also excel.

One idea must be reinforced: There are no right or wrong characteristics, no good or bad characteristics. We are where we are and what we are because of what has gone into our minds. We change where we are and what we are by changing what goes into our minds. Don't be satisfied with the broad generalities we are forced to work with in this book. If this area of personality characteristics interests you, contact us for more information on how to implement personality profiles.[1]

Let me emphasize again: There is no wrong character for management and no wrong type for achievement and Top Performance. Every profession seems to have its stereotypes—hard-driving, goal-oriented stockbrokers; laid-back, people-oriented social workers, etc.—and you may want to take those stereotypes into consideration when making career or employment choices. Yet even though different industries or companies may tend to be dominated by a particular type of personality, you will find variations and degrees everywhere. Remind yourself that different management styles are appropriate to different times and situations. If you are directing the fire drill, don't call for a consensus vote on exit plans. But don't grimly demand that people be creative in a brainstorming session either. Their ideas will simply dry up.

One of the men who best exemplifies the correct combination of all the characteristics we have been sharing in this chapter is the late Robert W. Woodruff of Coca-Cola. He was nicknamed "Mr. Anonymous" despite being the CEO of the Coca-Cola Company. Here is the text of a leaflet he carried in his pocket that summarizes a solid business and personal philosophy.

Life is pretty much a selling job. Whether we succeed or fail is largely a matter of how well we motivate the human beings with whom we deal to buy us and what we have to offer.

Success or failure in this job is thus essentially a matter of human relationships.

It is a matter of the kind of reaction to us by our family members, customers, employers, employees, and fellow workers and associates. If this reaction is favorable we are quite likely to succeed. If the reaction is unfavorable we are doomed.

The deadly sin in our relationships with people is that we take them for granted. We do not make an active and continuous effort to do and say the things that will make them like us, and believe in us, and trust us, and that will create in them the desire to work with us in the attainment of our desires and purposes. Again and again we see both individuals and organizations perform only to a small degree of their potential success, or to fail entirely, simply because of their neglect of the human element in business and life. *They take people and their reactions for granted. Yet it is these people and their responses that make or break them.*

It is believed that these words are those of Mr. Woodruff's friend Bernard F. Gimbel, the late chairman of Gimbel Brothers Inc. So greatly was he impressed by the message in these words that he had the pamphlet reprinted to pass out among the key people in his organization. You might say that over the years these words have almost become the spirit of Coca-Cola. These are words that all Top Performers would do well to live by.

PERFORMANCE PRINCIPLES

1. The more I understand myself, the more effectively I can work with others.
2. Personality profiles are valuable tools for getting the round pegs into the round holes and the square pegs into the square holes.
3. Self-evaluation (with a scientific tool) is more valuable than self-condemnation.
4. Our weaknesses are often extensions of our strengths.
5. There are no good/bad, right/wrong profiles—they simply help us evaluate where we are so we can determine where we want to go.
6. You are what you are and where you are because of what has gone into your mind; you change what you are and where you are by changing what goes into your mind.

13

Management Gems

Find the essence of each situation, like a logger clearing a logjam. The pro climbs a tall tree and locates the key log, blows it, and lets the stream do the rest. An amateur would start at the edge of the jam and move all the logs, eventually moving the key log. Both approaches work, but the "essence" concept saves time and effort. Almost all problems have a "key" log if we learn to find it.

Fred Smith

Throughout *Top Performance* we have made every effort to give credit where credit is due. We have painstakingly traced down every traceable bit of information to keep from claiming originality when there was none. In this final chapter in "The Science of Top Performance," we want to share with you some management gems that frankly are difficult to credit. These are timeless truths that have really been shared by most, if not all, effective managers. We are hopeful that you will find some "key logs" in these concepts and formulas that will answer your "opportunities" to solve problems more efficiently and effectively.

Formula for Top Performance Management

1. Show honest and sincere appreciation at every opportunity—make the other person feel important.
2. Don't criticize, condemn, or complain.
3. Make your cause bigger than your ego.
4. Work for progress, not perfection.
5. Be solution conscious, not problem oriented.
6. Invest time in the activity that brings the highest return on investment according to the priority list of responsibilities—effort alone doesn't count; results are the reasons for activity.
7. Fulfilling responsibility is a good reason for work; discipline is the method.
8. Recognize and accept your own weaknesses.
9. Make checklists and constantly refer to them.
10. *Always* show the people in your life the humility of gratitude.

Six Action Steps for Performance-Oriented Managers

1. Give regular, specific, and observable behavior feedback on performance.
2. Respect the lines of communication and authority.
3. Make timely decisions.
4. Be accessible.
5. Encourage creative ideas.
6. Provide personal support.

The Ten "Double Win" Rules That Lead to Top Team Performance

When dealing with others:

1. Remember that a *smile* is the most powerful social tool we have at our disposal.

2. Listening is the most neglected *skill* in business (or home) today. The person who listens controls the final outcome of the discussion. Encourage others to talk, and then consciously remove any barriers to your good listening skills.

3. Talk in terms of the other person's interests. You can find a "uniqueness" and "specialness" in every individual you meet. Others are interesting when these qualities are discovered; check out the other person's point of view.

4. Ask questions you already know the answer to and you will get to see the other person's perspective. Most ideas are more palatable if we "discover" them ourselves. People who truly care about others lead them down the "discovery path."

5. "What you are speaks so loudly I can't hear what you say." Remember to model the behavior and attitude you want the other person to have.

6. Give assignments that allow you to express faith and confidence that the other person can successfully perform in the task assigned.

7. Always make requests; never give orders.

8. Develop your ability to use the narrative story and the meaningful analogy—these are powerful teaching tools.

9. Always be respectful of others. Show your respect by being on time for meetings or letting others know why you must be late.

10. Return phone calls, emails, and letters immediately—there is no excuse for not doing so.

Exploding Some "Management Myths"

1. *Manipulation and motivation are often the same thing.* Absolutely not! Manipulation is getting people to act for you in ways that may not necessarily be for their own good. Motivation is helping people recognize mutual interests and getting them to join the cause because there is a benefit for them as well as you.

2. *Making your best effort is all that really counts.* No! Too many people substitute effort for accomplishment. The reason for working

is to get *results*. The person who gets the most results with less effort is working smarter and harder. Fatigue is not an indicator of success.

3. *Delegation is the key to management success.* Wrong again! Delegation is not telling someone what you want, when you want it, and how it is to be done; that is *direction*. Delegation means assigning the *results* you expect and designing a follow-up system that allows you to *in*spect what you *ex*pect. New employees get direction; experienced employees get delegation. Determining which employees need direction, giving it to them, and delegating results and the authority to get those results is an important key to management success.

4. *Managers are normally superior physically, mentally, and spiritually.* Nope! Very few managers are "normal"! And there is nothing in the books that says a manager is a "superior." Very simply put, managers are people willing to take responsibility and work through others to achieve results. Are you trying to be a "supervisor" or "superworker"?

5. *Managers must control all circumstances.* No way! Managers deal with problems and situations, and there is a distinct difference between the two. A situation exists because you cannot control it—people get ulcers trying to control the uncontrollable. A problem is something you can take action on. Excellent managers learn the difference between the two, take action on problems, and stop worrying about situations.

Your Challenge

There really are no "great revelations" in this brief summary chapter. However, professionals don't need to be told, but they are glad to be reminded. If you will read these few pages every day for twenty-one days, your career will be greatly enhanced by the principles you will be putting into action.

--- **PERFORMANCE PRINCIPLES** ---

1. Reread the principles listed in this chapter daily for twenty-one days!

PART 3

MOTIVATING THE
TOP
Performer

It is motive alone that gives character
to the actions of men.

Bruyere

14

The Ziglar Performance Formula

Tom Ziglar

Practice is the hardest part of learning, and training is the
essence of transformation.

Ann Voskamp

Performance, doing a job well, is a combination of attitude, effort, and
skill, all of which are influenced by the way management motivates employees. I have developed a mathematical formula based on this idea that I
believe illustrates the power of these three elements to motivate and inspire.
I call it the Ziglar Performance Formula.

$$\text{Attitude} \times \text{Effort} \times \text{Skill} = \text{Performance}$$
$$\text{A} \times \text{E} \times \text{S} = \text{P}$$

Have you ever wondered why the top 5 percent in almost every industry
will earn four, five, six, even seven times more than the average earner in
their industry? The Ziglar Performance Formula will clearly show you why
this is the case. Let's take a close look at what each word in the formula
represents.

Performance

This book is all about performance. Early in my career at Ziglar I came to a startling realization: Nobody buys training books, audio programs, or seminars. Instead, they are buying the *results* these programs will give them—which is increased performance! They believe what we teach can help them improve their performance and that this, in turn, will improve their results.

No matter what you do to earn money, the reality is that you are in the problem-solving business, and the better you perform, the more problems you will solve. Top Performance is all about solving problems.

A number of years ago, I took our company through the process of defining what we did as a business. Out of that exercise came the concept that we are in the "True Performance" business—we inspire and help individuals and companies achieve True Performance, which is really Top Performance with a spiritual foundation. We spent hours as a team coming up with a good and simple definition of True Performance: "*True Performance* is the ideal accomplishment of a goal, aspiration, or objective."

I was so proud of this definition that I immediately took it to Dad. I handed him the sheet of paper it was written on, and he read it to himself. He tilted his head and looked up for a moment and got out his pen. He then added four words that took the definition from good to better than good!

With a few strokes of the pen, Dad transformed an idealistic definition into a meaningful and measurable definition. True Performance is when you do the very best job possible and everyone wins. If this sounds vaguely familiar, compare it to the most famous of all Zig Ziglar quotes: "You can have everything in life you want if you will just help enough other people get what they want."

Simply put, when you complete a job, project, or sale, everyone must win in order for it to be considered True Performance. The customer, the

> "*True Performance* is the ideal accomplishment of a goal, aspiration, or objective that benefits everyone involved."

salesperson, the support team, the leadership of the company, and the community must all win. There are few things in life more satisfying than solving problems and achieving True Performance in the process.

Attitude

Attitude is the way you think or feel about someone or something. I believe our attitude is the outward expression of our character. It's normal to have a down moment or a bad day, but a perpetually bad attitude is something no one, and no business, can afford. How many times in your own experience have you stopped doing business with someone simply because of the attitude of the person you were dealing with? As Zig Ziglar said, "A positive attitude will outperform a negative attitude every time."

Effort

The right kind of effort is when you combine hustle and smarts. Effort that gets short-term and long-term results is planned out strategically and put into action with 100 percent focused attention. One hundred percent effort is not just a short burst of activity, which is great, but a commitment to see the project through long after the initial excitement is gone.

Skill

Skill is the ability to do something well. Great skill takes commitment to developing yourself to the best of your ability and comes after learning, training, repetition, and practice. Top Performers understand this and are constantly learning, training, and developing themselves and their teams.

The Ziglar Top Performance Formula

Following is a simple illustration of how the formula works in business. Imagine a new employee's first day on the job. Chances are good they have a lot of thoughts going through their mind:

Will I fit in?

Will the people here like me?

Will I mess up and get fired?

Will I be able to learn everything fast enough and do a good job?

As a leader of yourself and the people you influence, it is essential that you understand how attitude, effort, and skill impact each other. When a new employee walks in on their first day on the job, they have not yet been given any work to do; they are wondering if they will fit in, and they have not been given any specific skills training. This means, in the Ziglar Top Performance Formula, attitude is a 1, effort is a 1, and skill is a 1.

$$\text{Attitude} \times \text{Effort} \times \text{Skill} = \text{Performance}$$
$$1 \times 1 \times 1 = 1$$

Walking in, the new employee's performance score is 1.

Now imagine the new employee has a dynamic manager who says this to the new employee: "Thank you for being thirty minutes early. What a great way to start your first day on the job. I want you to know you are going to do fantastic here. Our whole team loves you! You did great in the interview process with each of our team members, and the assessments we did on you told us that you are perfect for this starting position. I believe that if you bring the right attitude, effort, and skill every single day, you will rapidly advance. Our whole team is ready to answer any questions you have. You have what it takes!

"Here is the schedule for your onboarding today. You will sit with each person on the team and they will share what they do and how you will be working with them. You will finish the day with HR. They will complete all your official paperwork, get you set up at your workstation, and answer any questions. Welcome aboard!"

Wow! It would be amazing if everyone's first day on the job were like this! If this were you, how would you feel? The right leader can have an amazing impact right out of the gate. In this scenario, the manager's words moved the new employee's attitude from a 1 to a 2 and the performance score doubled!

$$\text{Attitude} \times \text{Effort} \times \text{Skill} = \text{Performance}$$
$$2 \times 1 \times 1 = 2$$

Attitude improvement alone has doubled performance.

The reality is, at this point the manager has no fear of the new employee talking to one of her customers or prospects. She knows the positive attitude will more than make up for lack of skills or knowledge, and that if asked a question the new employee can't answer, the new employee will simply say with a big smile, "I am brand-new here. Let me find someone on our team who can help you."

Now imagine the second day on the job for the new employee. The manager who understands the Ziglar Top Performance Formula gives the new employee another positive talk to start the day and an assignment. The work to be done is straightforward, and the employee already has the skills necessary to do the work—for example, cleaning out a storage room and breaking down a bunch of boxes to be disposed of. Notice how performance doubles again.

$$\text{Attitude} \times \text{Effort} \times \text{Skill} = \text{Performance}$$
$$2 \times 2 \times 1 = 4$$

The business is now getting a return on their investment in the employee as the employee's performance increases. This is great for the new employee, but performance really starts to climb on day three. On day three, skills training starts and the employee learns new things specific to their job role. Suppose the primary role of the employee is phone-based customer support, and on day three the employee learns some simple phone scripts around the products and services the company offers and then begins to make follow-up calls to customers based on this new skill set. Now the employee is starting to make an impact with attitude, effort, and skill.

Performance has doubled again!

$$\text{Attitude} \times \text{Effort} \times \text{Skill} = \text{Performance}$$
$$2 \times 2 \times 2 = 8$$

I love sharing this scenario because it shows us how Top Performance really works. Now I have some good news and some bad news. The bad news is that the example I gave is where more than 90 percent of the world stops. The vast majority of people depend on their manager, their leader, their circumstances, or (you fill in the blank) to determine their attitude, effort, and skill. The good news is that some people choose the ownership mentality.

The Ownership Mentality

In order to achieve Top Performance and develop excellence in yourself and others, you need to choose the ownership mentality when it comes to your attitude, effort, and skill. In the scenario above, attitude, effort, and skill were positive because of a great manager. The ownership mentality means you don't depend on your manager, or anyone else, for your attitude, effort, and skill.

You own it!

You own your attitude. You don't care what kind of mood the people around you are in. You don't depend on your manager to lift your attitude. You don't care about the traffic or the weather. You have made the choice to have a fantastic attitude that is positively contagious, and you have created winning habits that keep your attitude positive. Your attitude, day in and day out, is a 3.

You own your effort. You don't care what the average is. It doesn't matter if you are cleaning out a storage room or working on a million-dollar project, you work smart and you give 100 percent effort. You always do a little bit extra, and you take time in planning and prioritizing your work day. Your effort, day in and day out, is a 3.

You own your skill. You appreciate the training your company provides, but you don't stop there. You are always going the extra mile to learn more, and you invest in yourself both personally and professionally. Your skill, day in and day out, is a 3.

When you apply the ownership mentality to the Ziglar Top Performance Formula, it looks like this:

Attitude	×	Effort	×	Skill	=	Performance
3	**×**	**3**	**×**	**3**	**=**	**27**

Now you know why the top 5 percent in almost every industry out-earn the average earners by so much! They own their attitude, effort, and skill.

As you can see, when you choose to own your attitude, effort, and skill, the possibilities are endless. You can always find ways to create more value and do just a little bit more. It is the addition of the little things that makes the big difference and takes your performance to the next level.

The Massive Impact of a Negative Attitude on Performance

Have you wondered what impact a negative attitude has on performance? It's huge! Let's plug a negative attitude into the Ziglar Top Performance Formula and see what happens. In a mathematical equation, when you change the value of an integer from positive to negative, the product of the equation also goes from positive to negative.

Attitude	×	Effort	×	Skill	=	Performance
–2	**×**	**2**	**×**	**2**	**=**	**–8**

That's right! A negative attitude changes the results from positive to negative. Here is what is even more worrisome. Suppose someone on the team has been there a long time, and they have terrific effort and skill, but they have a terrible attitude. Now look at the results:

Attitude	×	Effort	×	Skill	=	Performance
–2	**×**	**3**	**×**	**3**	**=**	**–18**

This type of employee is costing the company a fortune because they are infecting prospects, customers, employees, and vendors with their negative attitude. Many studies have shown that it is cheaper for a company to send a negative employee home with pay than it is to allow them to negatively impact the organization. Does this surprise you? I bet you are thinking of a few examples of this in your own life right now.

Presenting the Ziglar Top Performance Formula is one of the most powerful talks I give to corporations, because it makes the intangible tangible and demonstrates the real cost of a negative attitude and not having an ownership mentality when it comes to performance. The discussion and Q & A around this formula often dramatically impact the performance of the entire organization very quickly, just like it will impact your own performance very quickly.

The Sequence Is Important!

For some reason, sequence, or the importance of what comes first, is ignored in most businesses and academic institutions. Think about it. Almost every business starts training new hires on their skills first, then they give them work to do (effort), and then, when performance is lagging, they give them negative attitude incentives. No wonder so few in the marketplace have the ownership mentality.

In the Ziglar Performance Formula it is intentional that we start with attitude. Motivated employees have a great attitude that drives effort and increases skill, resulting in Top Performers!

PERFORMANCE PRINCIPLES

1. Attitude x Effort x Skill = Performance
2. Everyone must win.
3. Own your attitude.
4. Own your effort.
5. Own your skill.

15

A Formula for Motivation

You can't sweep people off their feet if you can't be swept off your own.

Clarence Day

One evening an associate and I flew back into Love Field in Dallas and got on the shuttle bus to take us to the outlying parking lot to pick up our car. As we stepped aboard, a client of mine warmly and enthusiastically greeted me. We exchanged a few pleasantries and then, to no one in particular and yet to everyone on the shuttle bus, he said, "From time to time I bring Zig in to talk to my organization. He's enthusiastic and optimistic, and he gets 'em all charged up and convinces 'em that everything's going to be fine and that they need to have a good, positive mental attitude." Then he continued by saying, "Of course, I look at things a little bit differently. I tell 'em exactly how it is and from time to time I chew 'em out pretty good!"

A passenger on the bus entered the conversation at that point and said, "In other words, Ziglar is unrealistic because he's so optimistic, and you're realistic in your approach." With this, I turned to the passenger and said, "Friend, let me ask you a question. What percentage of the bad things you expect to happen actually happen?" At that point another passenger entered the conversation and said, "About 5 or 10 percent of them." Then

I commented, "In other words, over 90 percent of the time the expected negative events just don't happen. This is realistic *and*, according to the experts, factual. From my perspective, the conclusion is obvious. *It's completely unrealistic to be negative and totally realistic to be positive.*"

However, it is unrealistic to deny that problems do exist, so let's take a serious look at a major problem and then look at some positive solutions.

Bridging the Gap

A general trend in business over the past number of years has been growing employee dissatisfaction, according to many of the research associations and newsmagazines that study business climate. Workers at all levels— hourly, clerical, professional, and even managerial personnel—are down on employers. Gripes have less to do with money and more to do with the work environment.

Now if you are wondering what this less than cheerful news is doing in such a positive book, let me explain that we should look for the positive in all situations. However, that must not keep us from identifying obstacles to becoming even more positive. Until and unless you specifically identify the problem in a company, you cannot solve it any more than your doctor could successfully treat you for an illness without first correctly identifying the illness. Identifying obstacles or problems is critical. *The key is to be solution conscious and not problem oriented.*

Use the following list of action steps to decrease employee dissatisfaction and increase good employee/employer relationships.

> *Show respect for a job well done.* Get rid of second-class job status regardless of pay differences. Real job equality is feeling we have a stake in our company's success.
>
> *Involve employees.* This means providing them with opportunities to make decisions and give useful input. This does not mean surrendering basic decision-making powers. It does mean giving employees a chance to participate, to be involved, *and* to be held accountable.

As a company leader, keep skid chains on your tongue. Talking about others may be destructive and probably is just gossip unless it's specifically designed to help.

Cultivate a calm, persuasive voice. How you say it is often more important than *what* you say. In any type of discussion or confrontation, your objective is to "win them over," not "win over them."

Make certain you are short on promises to your people and long on fulfillment. Actions do speak louder than words.

Be interested in the goals, welfare, homes, and families of those with whom you work. People have many facets in their lives. Don't be a one-dimensional supervisor. You may not supervise their private lives, but you can let them know you *really care.*

Keep an open mind on all debatable questions. Being the boss doesn't necessarily mean you are always right. Discuss but don't argue. The mark of a superior mind is the ability to disagree without being disagreeable.

Be careful of employees' feelings. Sarcasm, put-downs, and any form of ethnic or racial digs are no-nos. Leaders instinctively know that when someone is resentful and has a chip on their shoulder, the best way to remove the chip is to let that person take a bow.

Since employee morale is affected by many factors in and outside the workplace, those who have confidence in management's integrity are most likely to deliver their best work and to do so consistently. The best way management can build this confidence in itself is to communicate its abilities honestly, confidently, and directly. A well-run company is the best employee morale builder available.

In summary, what the researchers and their statistics say is very important; however, what they *don't* say is even more important: What the workforce really wants is management leadership whose competence and concern they can trust.

Workers desire and feel they deserve an opportunity to grow mentally, socially, spiritually, and physically, while sharing in the financial recognition and security rewards that come as a result of their growth and effort as part of the team.

Andrew Carnegie once said, "A man can succeed at almost anything for which he has unlimited enthusiasm." Regardless of how we define unlimited enthusiasm, it usually includes motivation, desire, drive, optimism, hope, faith, and energy. *People who are unable to motivate themselves must be content with the status quo no matter how impressive their résumé looks.* Now let's take a sobering look at why he made that statement and why motivation is a must in our personal and corporate lives.

Our Wasted Time

One shocking statistic that costs American businesses a great deal of money and countless opportunities is the incredible amount of time that is wasted, or even stolen. An August 1999 report by Michael G. Kessler & Associates showed that a survey of over five hundred employees across the nation found that almost 87 percent of those surveyed admitted to falsifying time sheets. While that is incredibly disturbing, an even greater form of time theft takes place every day without a second thought or even a sense of wrongdoing. The internet, though it has innumerable benefits, has the ability to eat into the productivity of almost every person who uses a computer and has web access. An estimated 38 percent of emails either are unwanted spam or don't pertain to the work at hand. Add this loss of time to the typical time wasters—water fountain discussions, late arrivals, early departures, personal phone conversations—and you have enough dollars lost through wasted time to potentially cause one out of three new businesses to fail. That's a lot of corporate dollars. But the truly big loss is the individual's, because Ralph Waldo Emerson was right when he said, "The right performance of this hour's duties will be the best preparation for the hours or ages that follow it."

> What the workforce really wants is management leadership whose competence and concern they can trust.

The most conservative nationwide survey I saw while compiling this information revealed that the average worker wastes nine full workweeks a year simply putting off or postponing work that should be done. Burke Marketing Research conducted the survey for Accountemps, an accounting, bookkeeping, and data-processing personnel organization. The survey was based on interviews with vice presidents and personnel directors of one hundred of America's one thousand largest companies. Those responding to the survey estimated that the average employee procrastinates 18 percent of the time, or nine full thirty-five-hour workweeks each year. Why? Well, the last survey question was: "What do you believe are the main reasons for procrastination in business?" The answers make up the following list. Read it and see if you agree that motivation could be the most important ingredient leadership can bring to a company.

Lack of communication

Low morale

Lack of interest in the job or particular task

Absence of clear-cut goals or objectives

Lack of discipline

Poor self-esteem

To this list we must add the thought that far too many people get carried away with what Charles E. Hammel identifies as the "tyranny of the urgent" and permit the "urgent" things to crowd out the "important" things. Basically, we have a *prioritizing* problem and not a *time* problem.

The proper utilization of our time and resources, according to Thomas K. Connellan, president of the Connellan Group of Ann Arbor, Michigan, involves some truths that are so simple and basic that many people miss them completely. First, we need to understand that there is no point in doing well that which you should not be doing at all. According to

Efficiency is doing things right.

Effectiveness is doing the right things.

Connellan, 10 to 15 percent of the tasks managers are personally handling should be delegated and 10 to 15 percent should be eliminated. When you take on a task, you should ask yourself if this is something you should be doing or something someone else should be doing. Focus on effective use of time rather than efficient use of time.

Question: What happens to these effective people who take their jobs seriously and use their time wisely? Answer: According to an Associated Press release from 1985, they get promoted.

> CHICAGO–Dull people may not be the first invited to parties, but they are usually the first in line for promotion, according to a research team at a medical college here. The team made a study of eighty-eight executives and found that those people with a "low pleasure capacity" make the most successful executives. This is because they can concentrate on their work without being distracted. . . . Executives who were categorized as "fun seeking" tended to have lower salaries. [Author's note: The key word is *seeking*. You should, even must, enjoy your work and have fun performing your job.]

The Successful Know about Attitude

Allan Cox, author of the widely acclaimed book *Confessions of a Corporate Headhunter*, talks a great deal about attitude and, as a result of a survey of 1,173 executives in thirteen corporations, has some strong opinions and factual information. He says, "Attitude determines strength. It determines direction. American executives by and large believe that having a positive attitude is responsible for career advancement." In his survey he asked the question, "What was your finding concerning the impact of positive thinking?" Among top executives, 49 percent said it affected their own success very strongly and 46.5 percent said it was a "significant" factor. In a nutshell, 95.5 percent of these men and women said their attitude played a very strong or significant part in their success. The rest were neutral on the question. On the other side, Cox points out that *no one with whom leaders deal is given less time and consideration than the negative thinker.*

Cox points out that positive thinking is not manipulating or being manipulated. It is not being grandiose; it is not being naïve. It is not being falsely enthusiastic or optimistic. Most important, perhaps, it is not denying periodic, normal bouts of discouragement. Thinking positively is not legislated experience either. By this he means you cannot practice it merely because someone tells you to, nor can you extend it selectively, say to life at home, and exclude it from work. He points out that life constantly presents us with obstacles and opportunities. Positive thinking is the means for dealing constructively with both.

An Important Gift You Can Give Others

One of the most important and positive things we can give others is *hope* with direction, encouragement, and believability—hope that the future is going to be bright for them regardless of where they are at the moment. Never will I forget an incident at a hotel on Marco Island, Florida, several years ago. A speaker friend and I were visiting in my room when a housekeeping staff member knocked and asked permission to clean the room. Since this did not present a problem, we invited her to go ahead.

She had been working less than a minute when our conversation stopped and I started watching her in action. Though she was substantially overweight, she moved with amazing speed. In three fast movements she stripped the blanket and linens from the bed. With each of her hands working, she removed the pillowcases from both pillows simultaneously. She took the sheet that covers the mattress and quickly put it on one side. Next she put on the top sheet, followed by the light blanket and the bedspread. Then she put the pillowcase on the pillow and completed that one side of the bed.

At that point she quickly moved to the other side and finished that side of the bed in record time. How she handled the next little maneuver is an absolute mystery to me, but somehow from the opposite side of the bed she flipped the bedspread and the pillow (which she had neatly tucked on the other side) over in the correct spot and, with two more quick movements on her side, the bed was complete.

I don't exaggerate when I say she made that bed in less than half the time of anyone I have ever seen. Since I served two years in the Navy and made a few hundred bunks myself, I consider myself knowledgeable on the subject. But this woman was far and away the best I've ever seen.

Curiosity demanded that I get some information, so I asked her whether she minded if I asked her some questions. She cheerfully responded, "No, go right ahead," but in the meantime she was doing the other things needed to clean the room. First I asked her whether she worked on an hourly basis or if she was paid by the room. She told me she was paid by the room. I smilingly asked, "I'll bet you do all right, don't you?" For the first time she stopped and said, "Well, to tell you the truth, I have a large family and I am the only one to support them, so I have to work hard." Then she grinned from ear to ear and said, "And yes, I do all right."

Where You Start Is Not Important

I wish I could complete this story by saying I got her name and address and two years later I discovered she was the manager of the hotel. Unfortunately—and for me, amazingly—I did not even get her address, so I cannot finish her story on that kind of note. However, I'll bet she's still doing "all right."

About a year later I was speaking in Zanesville, Ohio, and had lunch with the manager of a Holiday Inn and the president of the Chamber of Commerce, along with a personal friend. As we visited, I told the story of this woman, and the manager of the Holiday Inn said, "Well, obviously that was not me, but it could have been." She pointed out that when she finished high school, she got married and had to go to work. The only job available was to serve as the housekeeper at the Holiday Inn, and her job was cleaning rooms. However, she determined that she was going to work as hard as possible and be the best at what she did. The net result was that within six months she was manager of that floor of the Holiday Inn. A few months later she was manager of the entire housekeeping department. About a year later they moved her into the restaurant, first as assistant manager and shortly after as manager. A couple of years later she was manager of the Holiday Inn in Zanesville, Ohio, and served in that capacity for several years. This woman, Nan Gump, could easily have been immobilized by where she had to start. Instead, she realized that *where you finish* is much more important.

> Can you train motivation so that it lasts and has an impact?

Can Motivation Affect Where You Finish?

My dream to be a professional speaker started in 1952, but it was not until 1970 that I could pursue my dream on a full-time basis. It was 1972 before my speaking career really exploded. During the course of the preparation for what was to be, I always stayed grounded in my philosophy and the principles I adhere to. I altered ways in which I delivered the training in those early years, but I was fixated on the principles.

In the mid-sixties I was educating organizations on sales training principles with the underlying brand of motivation that has become the identity of Ziglar Inc. In the course of those relationships, I met a young man named Larry Proffit. Larry decided to take some of the principles I taught, along with his own experiences and expertise, and go to Japan to expand his horizons. Larry succeeded in culturally translating those principles with the help of his literary translator, a Japanese gentleman named Tom Watanabe. Tom Watanabe had a relationship with another Japanese gentleman named Mr. Masuda. The story takes a turn when these two Japanese gentlemen joined hands in a project that would bring Watanabe to the United States. Larry Proffit was invited to join the organization as the person in charge of sales and sales training. Today the company is a multibillion-dollar direct-marketing company based in Irvine, California, called Nikken.

Almost thirty years after our first encounter, Larry decided to invite me to speak for this giant corporation at their convention in San Francisco. There I was introduced to a young Korean gentleman named Kendall Cho, who was the vice president of finance for Nikken. The next five years moved even more quickly as the relationship solidified. Ziglar Inc. and Nikken developed a couple of custom training programs, and I made a few more personal appearances at their annual conventions. In 2001 Nikken invited me to become their international honorary chairman and national spokesperson. As I look back on the cycle of events of those thirty-five years, I am more convinced than ever that success comes to those who are not only determined but also consistent.

My symbol of persistence for the last three and a half decades has been a chrome-plated water pump, and those of you who know that story know that my message is to keep on pumping after you have primed the pump.

At first you have to pump vigorously, and when the water starts to flow, all you have to do is maintain a slow, steady pace. Those early years of pumping have paid off in ways that are indescribable, but the icing on the proverbial cake is that in Nikken's recognition system, he used various lapel pins to give recognition to employees, and the first pin rank was a small water pump designed as a lapel pin. Ironically, employees at Ziglar Inc. also receive one of those pins when they finish a year of service with us.

Yes, motivation can and does impact where you finish in life.

Can You "Stand" Motivated?

Of all the subjects on this earth, surely one of the most exciting and confusing is the subject of motivation. The next example opens the door and deals with just one facet of this intriguing subject.

I don't know how you "stand" when you're waiting in a line or waiting for something to happen, but I will never forget a little incident that took place in Washington, DC, that fairly well describes the average person's concept of what motivation is and what a motivated person does. I had spoken for the National Federation of Parents for Drug-Free Youth, and the response had been very gratifying. The audience laughed at the appropriate places, nodded in agreement at the right spots, applauded at the high spots, and gave me an enthusiastic standing ovation when it was all over. Compliments flowed thick and fast. Had my wife been there, she would have loved everything they said about me! My children would have been a little embarrassed about it, and my mother would have *believed* every word. In short, it was an "up" occasion for me.

The next morning I was in the restaurant waiting for the host to seat the guest who preceded me. I was quietly standing, awaiting his return. As I stood there, three women who had been present at my talk the night before joined the people who were waiting in line behind me. These three women obviously thought I was out of earshot or would not be tuned in to what they were saying. However, here's the conversation I picked up. First woman: "There is our speaker from last night." Second woman: "Yes, and he is obviously a 'night' person!" Third woman: "He must be, because he sure doesn't look motivated to me!"

Now to be really honest, I don't know how you either "look" motivated or "stand" motivated. I suppose the women thought I should have had an ear-to-ear grin on my face, or perhaps I should have been bouncing up and down and waving to the people in the restaurant. If that's their idea of a motivated person, all I can say is that they are way, way off base.

The question I am most often asked is, "Are you always so 'up'?" And the answer, of course, is, "No, I'm not *always* 'up.'" But I am "up" about 95 percent of the time. Usually if I am not "up," it is because I am exhausted as a result of a grueling schedule. Common sense and experience then dictate to me that I need to either take a nap or go for a walk—which is exactly what I do if it's humanly possible.

I should explain, however, that there is a vast difference between being "up" and being "on." Anyone who is "on" twenty-four hours a day is "on" something that is deadly! In short order that person will suffer from burnout and probably end up as a depressed, perhaps even psychotic, individual. Either that or efforts to always be "on" could lead to a tragic dependency on drugs, which have claimed far too many (even one is too many) people who are deluded into believing that they must always be "on" and having a marvelous time.

Just Who Is Motivated?

Unfortunately, too many people think of the "motivated" person as the loudly enthusiastic, turned-on extrovert who is making noise and is the center of attention, whether that person is in a crowd of ten or ten thousand. This is not necessarily motivation; it probably falls under the banner of "hysteria," and hysteria is giving motivation a bad reputation. I'm not saying that the extrovert is not motivated, because they *could* be, but being loud certainly doesn't necessarily mean being motivated. Some of the most "up" and motivated people I've ever known are quiet and unassuming. Obvious point: You can be "up" and motivated while quietly jogging, reading, praying, thinking, holding hands with your mate, or even sleeping.

As I wrote that last paragraph, the Redhead was waiting to take a walk in the botanical gardens along the Brisbane River in Brisbane, Australia. What an "up" experience it was! The greenery, shrubs, flowers, rocks, plants, birds, boats, water, and people were beautiful, fascinating, and quiet. At no time during the walk would anyone have accused us of being "on," especially when we sat on the bench to watch the ducks and birds in their never-ending quest for food. However, it was definitely an "up" experience and is permanently recorded in my memory bank as a most enjoyable, motivating interlude.

I might also add that taking a break to relax and meditate helps to clean out the garbage and the cobwebs from the yesterdays of life so that you really are clearing the decks for more effective action today. Another benefit is that this kind of *meditation* will help eliminate lots of *medication.*

Yes, life can be—even *should* be—sprinkled from time to time with "up" experiences. For me, a walk with one of my children or grandchildren, a game of golf with my wife or son, a moving sermon, inspiring semiclassical music, a hymn of the faith, or a drama about real life depicting the good guy winning over the bad guy is always an "up" experience. These events turn me on when I need to be turned on to do the speaking and writing that my profession requires.

My guess is you are pretty much the same way and, like me, you have certain things that *do not* get you as motivated as your best performance demands. It may be a certain aspect of your job, such as paperwork or long and tedious meetings. It may be making cold calls on unmotivated buyers. It may be dealing with and trying to manage other people's frustrations when you feel you have enough of your own aggravations to last a lifetime. The question should be, "Is it possible to be motivated about something that I am *not* motivated about right now?" The answer is a definite Yes! Especially if you understand that most small problems, when nourished with procrastination, will grow bigger and bigger.

Before we really get into this concept of motivation, let me make one more point. You may be as motivated as you ever want to be. The chances are good, however, that there is someone in your life who is not as motivated as you would like him or her to be. So as you read the next chapters, don't forget that you are reading from two perspectives: (1) How will this information help me to be a Top Performer? and (2) How will this information help me to help others be Top Performers? You will be pleased with the answers you find to both questions—I guarantee it!

PERFORMANCE PRINCIPLES

1. You must understand motivation to motivate others consistently.
2. Management's imperative is to cultivate its human resources.
3. What the workforce really wants is management leadership whose competence and concern they can trust.
4. One of the most important things we can give others is hope with direction, encouragement, and believability.
5. Where you start is not as important as where you finish.
6. You can be "up" without being "on."

16

Why You Manage— Why They Follow

The true motives of our actions, like the real pipes of an organ, are usually concealed. But the gilded and the hollow pretext is pompously placed in the front for show.

Charles Caleb Colton

AWARENESS
ASSUMPTIONS
ANALYSIS
ACTION

The first *A* in our Four-A Formula to develop motivation over the next four chapters stands for *Awareness*. When I am talking about awareness, I am talking about answering the question *Why?* Why are you reading this book? Why are you continuing to work in your job? Why are you continuing to be involved in the day-to-day activities that fill your life? The *honest* answer to the question *Why?* is also the answer to your *personal* motivation. This is not motivation that has been imposed on you by anyone else; it's your personal motivation. One of the early success writers suggested we take the word *motivation* and make a slash between the *v* and the *a*—and if you've got just a little bit of imagination, you can see two words.

motiv/ation

The word on the left is *motive*, and the word on the right is *action*. People who are motivated have a motive; they have a reason, a purpose, or a cause. And then they take action on that reason, purpose, or cause. Question: *Have you given it any thought at all?*

My friend Ray, while attending college, was placed in a 7:30 a.m. English class that met on Saturdays. In his words, "The counselors saw me coming, didn't they? They must have said, 'This guy looks like he just fell off the turnip truck! Let's put him in that 7:30 a.m. Saturday English class and he'll probably show up!' They did—and I did!"

He went on to tell me that the teacher walked to the front of the room and immediately gave an assignment. The class was to write a short theme on "Why I Am Going to College." The students dutifully got down to business, but after about ten minutes, Ray got up and left the room. When the class was over, several of his friends walked out to the quadrangle to find him. Sure enough, Ray was sitting in front of the library. "Ray, what are you doing?" his puzzled friends asked.

"Funny, I never thought about it before," Ray said, "but I don't want to go to college! The only reason I'm here is that you guys are here, and my other friends are here, and my mom and dad wanted me to go to college. I don't want to go to college. I want to go to work at the plant where my dad works, get married, have a family, play slow-pitch softball at night, and spend time with my family on the weekends. I just never thought about it until that teacher asked the question."

The real irony of this true story is that Ray was a straight-A student in high school, and chances are good he could have gone on to be whatever he studied to be. However, with that attitude, he would have been a mediocre doctor, lawyer, scientist, teacher, manager, or anything else. He would have been mediocre because he had not identified his own personal reasons, purposes, or causes. If we are to motivate ourselves, we must honestly face up to the real reasons we do the things we do.

If we want to motivate other people, we have got to find out what their reason, purpose, or cause is. People are not going to be motivated for *your* reasons. They are going to be motivated for their own reasons. We must understand that *everyone* listens to the *same* radio station. The station is WII-FM, and the call letters stand for What's In It For Me? If you want to motivate others, this is the information you need to share. You've got to find out their motive, reason, and cause—and then use those to encourage them to take action.

The first time you attempt to discover what another person's motives are, you will probably get an answer he or she thinks you would like to hear. If you continue to probe, you will get an answer that someone very close to that person would like to hear. And if you continue to probe, you might get the *truth*. Now people don't mean to be deceitful. It's just that they haven't given much thought to what really is important to them. Money is not a motivator—what we *can do with the money* is what really motivates others and us. Whether it's the biggest home on the street or the largest donation to the orphanage, our motives vary greatly.

Types of Motivation

Honest realization of our motives (or those of others) is the first step in understanding motivation. Motivation comes in three forms: (1) fear, (2) incentive, and (3) change or growth.

Fear Motivation

Fear motivation works for some people some of the time. In most cases it is temporary, but there are occasions when it is effective. When the economy is extremely tight and there are more workers than jobs, many workers will consciously make a much greater effort to be extremely productive in an effort to ensure their jobs. They will arrive earlier, stay later, and do more while they are there. However, if this is their only motive, the chances are excellent that over a period of time they will grow weary of well-doing and revert back to their old habits and, if the economy is still bad, will ultimately end up losing their jobs. Temporarily, however, it will work and effect an increase in productivity for them.

In the marketplace, fear motivation sometimes is temporarily effective to keep workers in line and to help them become team players and cooperate with, and on occasion even be subservient to, their superiors. But again, the results are temporary and over the long haul can even backfire.

Incentive Motivation

The second kind of motivation is *incentive motivation*. All of us have seen the familiar picture of the donkey pulling the cart with a carrot dangling in front of him. The donkey's motivation to pull is obviously to reach and take a bite of that carrot. For this incentive to work, the load has got to be light enough for him to pull, the donkey's got to be hungry enough so that he wants to take a bite of that carrot, and the carrot has got to be desirable enough to appeal to him. However, if he does not eventually have his bite of carrot, he's going to recognize that it's a "con game," and he will stop pulling.

The only problem is, when you give the donkey a big enough bite of the carrot, he is no longer going to be hungry and, consequently, his motivation to pull is dramatically reduced. At this point, the only way you can get him to pull is to lighten the load, shorten the stick, and sweeten the carrot. The problem here is that in the business world we have a load that is fairly well dictated by market conditions and, if you lighten it too much, or if you give the donkey too big a bite of the carrot (or the profit generated by the free enterprise system), the operation is no longer profitable and we ultimately end up out of business. Remember: Today's fringe benefits are tomorrow's expectations. So what do you do? Answer: Change the donkey to a thoroughbred and make him *want* to run.

Change or Growth Motivation

This brings us to the third kind of motivation, which is *growth motivation*. The primary purpose of growth motivation is to change the thinking, the capacity, and the motivation of the workers. We must make them want to pull that cart (do their job). We must give them reasons for doing what we want them to do and what *they* want to do. In other words, we must work with employees to the degree that we can help them get the things they want in life. That's a major purpose of *Top Performance*: to give specific

171

methods, procedures, and techniques for helping each individual grow and inspire them so they will want to do a better job—not just for the benefit of the company but for their own benefit as well. As I've said before, in reality we are all "on the same team," and, consequently, we have the same objectives. When management and labor both clearly understand that they are on the same side, then both sides will be willing, even eager, to cooperate.

When I was a small boy, my friends and I frequently walked on an abandoned section of the railroad tracks. Each of us attempted to keep our balance and walk the farthest, but inevitably, after a few steps we would fall. Had we but realized it, two of us could have gotten on opposite rails, reached across, and held hands and, together, walked indefinitely.

I'm convinced that in the business world when management and labor, employer and employee, fully understand that they are on the same side and have the same objectives, if they will "hold hands" and work together, all will benefit. Then we are not only developing our maximum potential as individuals, but we're also achieving the maximum productivity in our company, which ensures the stability and growth of that company. That's the kind of thinking and motivation that will bring optimum results and permanent benefits for labor and management.

I'm convinced that everyone is motivated at some time in his or her life about something. Winners are motivated a high percentage of the time. *Winning leaders* are motivated most of the time, and almost always when the chips are down. My friend the late Gene Lewis, one of the great commonsense leaders I had the privilege to work with, shared this analogy that clearly points out what happens to entirely too many people:

> A glowworm does its fishing not in water, but in the air. It spins and lets down fine glutinous threads. When a gnat or other small insect, attracted by the light, collides with one of these strange fishing lines, it is caught and held. The glowworm reels in the line and consumes the captive. If its hunger is satisfied, the glowworm puts out its light. Otherwise, it drops another line for another tidbit. The soft light that gives the glowworm its unearthly beauty is not produced by the "contented" glowworm. The scintillating lights come from the glowworms that are hungry and indeed earnest about their fishing.
>
> Unique creatures though they are, these glowworms have qualities in common with human beings. With us, as with them, the full stomach too often brings about a state of complacency that dims desire for accomplishment.

The young man starting out in life is spurred on by powerful "bread and butter" incentives. To be sure of eating regularly, he must pass certain tests. He must be able to master the fundamentals of his business and to adapt himself to the conditions that make for success in that business. Hungry with desire for life's necessities, he "fishes" in that business in dead earnest, and if he has the right qualities, his "glow" attracts success.

But, after he has met with a measure of success, he faces a different kind of test. Is he still impelled by a strong inner drive to fish hard for the really big stakes?

Many who pass the initial tests brilliantly are stopped by this secondary test. They stall at the top of the first hill. They are so eager to enjoy the fruits of their success that they are unwilling to put forth the efforts to augment their education, acquire specialized training, or do whatever else may be necessary to reach still greater heights of service and personal advancement.

Obviously, Gene is not talking about *leaders* in that last paragraph. True leaders who are really motivated will use one success to build to an even bigger one. Leaders know that they are the example their subordinates look to for guidance and direction. *As managers, they know they'll be measured and judged by the number of their subordinates who surpass them.* They clearly understand that the mark of greatness is the ability to develop it in others.

Krish Dhanam had the good fortune to meet one of the world's greatest management leaders. He tells the story:

Saintly Leadership

On June 7, 1994, I had the rare privilege of meeting one of the most effective Top Performers of our time. I was entrusted with the task of taking a donation from my employer in Dallas to a little missionary worker in the slums of Calcutta. I was asked to meet and greet Mother Teresa and offer the donation as a gesture of goodwill for all that she had accomplished. Little did I know that the twenty-minute encounter would give me some incredible leadership principles that would last me a lifetime.

In my haste to part with the money and capture a picture with the future saint, I kept egging this icon of patience to come to where I was standing so a memory of our meeting could be recorded. It was clearly evident from what transpired that the memory I wanted to create was not as significant as the result of the actions of that day. My camera stopped working, and all efforts to get a picture were thwarted by fate, coincidence, or happenstance.

I left India disappointed and blamed myself for coming so close to greatness and failing to get a picture, but the saintly leadership of Mother Teresa taught me some valuable lessons.

She was consistent in her quest to save the very poor, calling them "distress in disguise." In an audio series called Thirsting for God, she told of the many times when she faced the impossible only to be rewarded because of her consistency.

She was loyal to her cause. Her acceptance speech when receiving the Nobel Peace Prize was simply, "I accept this in the name of the poor." These were the people she was called to lead, and amid the degradation and decadence of human decay, she found the self-reliance to be loyal to her cause.

She believed in succession planning. Even though the world knew her name and her deeds, she knew that one day her role as the visionary for the Missionaries of Charity would end. She knew that she needed a successor whose vision could take this humble organization forward. Sister Nirmala was appointed as successor the day Mother Teresa passed on, and continuity was established.

The role of Top Performers is to learn the various attributes that allow people to go from normalcy to greatness. Great people don't start out to be great. They follow their vision with consistency and loyalty.

When I wrote a letter of gratitude to Mother Teresa, she replied with a picture and a personal note to me. She taught me humility. This great lady wrote me a letter thanking me for mailing some letters for her that were sent to encourage the sisters representing the Missionaries of Charity in the US. Along with the picture and letter were the words, "Be a little instrument in God's hands, so that He can use you any time, anywhere. We have only to say 'Yes' to Him. The poor need your love and care. Give them your hands to serve, and your heart to love. And in doing so, you will receive much more. Keep the joy of loving through serving." In doing this she proved to be a great encourager.

I called this segment "Saintly Leadership" because most of us know that she got her skills at a venue more prestigious than Harvard and from a teacher who was called just that—Teacher. I call her a Top Performer because this Roman Catholic nun, who lived and served amid the poorest of the poor, made her home in the only Marxist state in a predominantly Hindu society. Dominique Lappierre called this infested maze of degradation and filth "The City of Joy." Yet when Mother Teresa died, she was given full state honors and was sent to her resting place on the gun carriage that carried some of the great martyrs of India. She transcended circumstances and societal assumptions and rose above the plateau of mortal expectations while practicing servant leadership of the very highest order. While many of us will not be called to live a life of such exemplary servitude, we can conclude that all Top Performers can practice the principles of saintly leadership.

A Most Misunderstood Ingredient

One of the points Krish's story about Mother Teresa makes indirectly is that if you are going to be a consistent Top Performer, it's important that you understand what happiness really is. Mother Teresa certainly understood true happiness. Many people maintain they'll be happy *when* . . . they win the trip to Hawaii, New York, or Bermuda. Many people say they'll be happy when they get the new house, but they won't. Then they'll be happy when the landscaping is completed, but they won't. Then they say they'll be happy when the new draperies are up—but that's not true either. Then they'll be happy when the mortgage is paid off, but again, they're wrong. They'll be happy when they've added the new room to the house, but that's not true. Then they'll be happy when they build that little place out by the lake—but again, it simply is not so.

Happiness is not a *where* or *when*—it is a *here* and *now*! It is not what you *have* that makes you happy; it is what you *are* that's going to make you happy! Material things are never going to make us happy. Adam and Eve had the whole world (including, as far as I know, the mineral rights). God gave them everything and authority over it—with the exception of one tree. He carefully instructed them not to eat the fruit of that tree. With all the material possessions they had, what was the one thing they wanted? You guessed it: the fruit of that tree.

Money and Position Won't Make You Happy

Many people say, "When I get a million dollars, then I'll be happy because I'll have security," but that's not necessarily so. Most people who acquire a million dollars want another million and then another. Or they could be like a good friend of mine who made and lost every dime of a million dollars. It didn't bother him a bit. He wasn't excited about it, but he explained to me, "Zig, I still know everything necessary to make another million dollars, and I've learned what to do not to lose it. I'll simply go back to work and earn it again." He proceeded to do exactly that—and more. No, security is not based on money. General Douglas MacArthur said that security lies in our ability to produce—and I believe he's right.

Many people say, "I'll be happy when I get to be head of the company because that represents security—when I'm the person in charge." That's not true. As you well know, even the best presidents will be out of a job in eight years. No, if we are to have happiness and security and continue to be motivated, we must understand that security comes from within. It lies in our ability to produce. In my mind, one of the best ways to be certain that we will continue to produce even when our needs have long ago been met is to continue to apply the principles and procedures we advocate in *Top Performance*.

───────────── **PERFORMANCE PRINCIPLES** ─────────────

1. Do you know why you do what you do?
2. Motivation = the motives we take action on.
3. Happiness is not a *where* or *when*—it is a *here* and *now*.
4. To motivate yourself, identify your motives and take action on them; to motivate others, identify their motives and use those to encourage them to take action.

17

Managing Productivity

A man without a purpose is like a ship without a rudder.

Thomas Carlyle

AWARENESS
ASSUMPTIONS
ANALYSIS
ACTION

The second *A* in our Four-A Formula stands for *Assumptions*. Krish Dhanam and Bryan Flanagan have provided the material for this topic. I found their insights to be profound, and I'm sure you will too. Having said that, Krish will kick off this chapter and Bryan will wrap it up.

Krish

Assumptions about people and their productivity are usually made after awareness and before analysis. Most managers make assumptions about the abilities and capabilities of the people they lead. These assumptions are usually based on opinions—opinions that are formed by a variety of observations that are seen, felt, and observed around the workplace.

Once I was conducting a training session for a company that was in an expansion mode. They had grown from using two floors of a five-story office building to using all five floors. When I was escorted to the second-floor training room where the presentation was scheduled to take place, I observed something unusual. The person who was escorting me started speaking in a lower tone as soon as we got off the elevator on the second floor. On inquiring as to why she was almost whispering, I learned something amazing. In the old configuration, the second floor of that building housed the executive offices, and it was customary to speak softly when on that floor. Everyone assumed they still needed to follow tradition.

To effectively motivate people, you have to deal with the assumptions about what is and what is not. The adage that in most organizations perception is fact and fact is never really fact rings true.

Assumptions can form in many different areas. We have outlined some for you so you can readily recognize them and lead your people to Top Performance in those respective areas.

Societal and Cultural Assumptions

In an increasingly cross-cultural world, there are many societal assumptions that hinder progress within an organization. A focus of the '80s and '90s was to sensitize the workplace and make it increasingly more tolerant to the changing demographics of our times. While politically correct terminology creates a platform of sensitivity in addressing people with differences, the more important need is to address the foundation of societal assumptions within work boundaries.

As a native of India, I have some assumptions about the American workplace, and this is reflected in the work ethic I choose. I have concluded beyond any reasonable doubt that the notion that anything is possible in America is true. This belief motivates me to do what I do in a different manner than someone who does not have the same socioeconomic and ethnic heritage as I do. I give my father, a retired executive in India, all the credit for this work ethic. For example, as director of international operations, I choose to come to work at 5:00 a.m. when I am in town and not on a training assignment. My philosophy is that if you provide real-time customer service in the international marketplace, this will set you apart from most of your competition. Except for the east coast of Australia, I can connect with most people around the globe in real time, taking into account the various time zones in the world. As a father and husband, this allows me to give an honest day's work and return home at 3:00 or 4:00 p.m., beating the traffic both ways, so I can enjoy my family.

If you were to try to motivate me just like you motivate everyone else in your organization, you would have missed the mark. As I've traveled around the world with Mr. Ziglar, he often asked me why I do not hesitate to do the things others would consider "lowly." My societal conditioning forces me to be grateful, and this is the prime reason. The secondary reason is that in all my time with Mr. Ziglar I have always felt special, because he respects my heritage. That is what Top Performers do. They know that while everyone is accountable for their future, no one is responsible for their heritage. Respecting a person's belief system will allow you to gain maximum productivity from them as they strive to do better for you and with you.

Experience-Based Assumptions

A résumé is written very carefully to articulate the significant things a person has already done before coming to you. Sometimes individuals stretch the truth to give the one looking at their candidacy a greater degree of optimism. This optimism is based on the experience a candidate brings to your organization and the immediate results this experience will produce. Leaders make many assumptions based on experience.

I once heard of a human resources manager who told a young applicant that if he were to logically add all the years of experience the candidate claimed in many different disciplines, he not only should have been retired but, barring modern scientific intervention, should have been dead. In other words, that candidate, like many others, had chosen to embellish and exaggerate his experiences.

Assumptions made based on a person's ability just because they claim to be experienced can cause leadership hardships. The effective way to navigate this hurdle is to assign people who claim knowledge to work with others who have already demonstrated it. Many leaders have paid the price of lost productivity because they entrusted too much to people who claimed that they could deliver because of their experience. In the true sense of teamwork, no one individual can accomplish the goals on their own. A salesperson who sold a million dollars' worth of logical software solutions might not be as successful selling an intangible service. While all sales processes can be learned, and product knowledge can be gained through effective training, it is often wise to look at a person's experience closely and make rational assignments instead of emotional ones.

Age and Gender Assumptions

Gray hair does not automatically signify wisdom any more than youth signifies ignorance. The workplace of today has changed quite drastically. Some ceilings do still exist, but assumptions of age and gender are not only illegal but also illogical in the leadership process. In order to be a Top Performer and get the best out of your employees, you have to encourage input from men and women of all ages.

As you motivate and lead your team and your organization, don't discount anyone's opinion purely on the basis of age or gender. Abraham Lincoln lost every election until he was over fifty years old, and he made his most significant contribution when he signed the Emancipation Proclamation in 1862 at the age of fifty-three. Senator John Glenn was the first to be hurled into space in a crude craft called the *Mercury* and then the oldest to fly a manned space mission aboard the shuttle. Bill Gates was a teenager when he decided to change the world. Within twenty-four hours of putting this book down, chances are you will utilize one of his ideas to make your life simpler. Everyone knows that Charles Lindbergh was the first person to cross the Atlantic by plane. Everyone also knows that Amelia Earhart was the first woman to cross the Atlantic, but few people know that she was also the second person ever to claim that impressive accomplishment.

Treat everyone equally and you will realize tremendous reward.

Personality-Based Assumptions

How often have you heard the statement, "She has a great personality," or "His demeanor and attitude are surely going to be a plus around these parts"? Personality-based assumptions have led to people getting assignments they are neither qualified for nor equipped to handle. Fred Smith said that in order to be effective, individuals have to put their talent before their passion. In the fast-paced world of the modern workplace, people's desire for more success may lead them to show an interest in or passion for some tough assignments that are beyond their true abilities. Unfortunately, some managers look for purely enthusiastic people like this instead of people with a blend of enthusiasm and the talent [or skills] necessary for the task.

Skill and will are both needed to ensure Top Performance. In the Ziglar offices we use personality-based assessments to find out an individual's strengths and weaknesses, and we then ensure that the assignments people receive are complemented by their strengths. If an individual is weak in an area, we encourage them to get strong in that area by identifying their knowledge gap.

Ensure that you have the right people for the right task by looking beyond the personality into the strengths and weaknesses of the individual. Assuming that because a person exhibits a certain personality they are best qualified for the task may lead to some discrepancies in productivity down the road and hurt the organization's goals. If we personally endorsed everyone who was motivated to work with us and become a speaker or trainer, as we are often requested to do, we would be reacting to the external traits that are displayed to us in the public arenas. But since consistency is what we require for people to represent our philosophy, we have a process in place. This process determines whether these individuals are truly interested in representing the philosophy and doing everything required for it, or whether they want to cash in on the goodwill and enjoy a couple of successful legs of the journey with us.

> If somebody has to tell you how good they are every step of the way, they probably are not.

Recently I met a fellow speaker who was interested in doing some work with us and had some unique ideas and methodologies that would really complement and supplement our own training programs. Realizing that I should not make a personality-based assumption, I informed the individual that in order to represent Ziglar, he needed to qualify through a process like everyone else. This individual proceeded to inform me that he was already very busy and would have to factor in time in his enormously active schedule to go through the qualification process, and that the standing ovations and references should be enough for us to consider him as an exception to the norm. He wanted us to make an assumption about his effectiveness because of what he told us and how he told us. I politely informed the young man that if he was so busy, then maybe we needed to work with him and get some work from him, because we were not that busy ourselves. Obviously I was joking, but in the process I made a point of not reacting to a personality-based assumption.

Bryan

I discovered the value of the "inner view" (a view that goes way beyond what seems obvious to me) when I was a sales manager with the IBM Corporation in California. I was with IBM's old typewriter and copier division at the time and had inherited fourteen salespeople when I took the job. I had been in the position for a few weeks when I asked one of my top sales representatives to step into my office.

I said, "John, I have been watching you for the past few weeks, and let me tell you how impressed I am with you, your professionalism, and your work ethic. Your production is great. You are over 125 percent of your quota, and you have a great forecast for next quarter. I'm also impressed with the reputation you have with your coworkers. The other reps respect you, and the administrative people think highly of you. You're going on my list of reps I'd like to promote. You could get to Boulder on the manufacturing side, or Dallas with marketing training, or even back East with financial planning. John, I really believe you could call the shots on your career path."

Then John said something that stopped me dead in my tracks. He said, "Bryan, are you talking about promoting me and relocating me? Is that what all this is about?" I assured him that was exactly what I had in mind. John then said, "You don't understand. I don't want to be promoted and leave the Bay Area. I love it here. Do you know what my goals are?" I replied that I really didn't know what John's goals were. I *assumed* it was to move up through the IBM career ranks, much like I was doing.

John said, "Let me tell you my goals. I want to raise my family right here in the Bay Area. My wife is from here, and my kids have great schools and friends. I don't want to uproot them and move away from here. I want to play slow-pitch softball and fish. I want to be a career sales professional. I don't want to move."

This had a big impact on me. I was offering something that my sales rep didn't want. I assumed that I knew John's goals. This is a big mistake that managers too often make.

This leads us to the value of conducting an *inner view*. The purpose of the *inner view* is to gain insights into your teammates so that you can assist them in reaching their goals and objectives. This requires time and dedication. It requires that you invest time getting to know your people as *people and not as units of production*! It requires that you dedicate yourself to understanding *their* needs, *their* issues, and *their* concerns.

Let me issue a caution. This process is not to be used in the place of a performance review or appraisal. It is also not to be used as a reprimand process. It is to be used to gain insights into your people so you can provide feedback and encouragement. There are three stages that work like this: First, you should schedule time with the individual. This can be done off-site at a coffee shop, at lunch, or at a neutral location in the office. Second, during the meeting you must condition yourself to *ask open-ended questions* and *listen to the responses*. You must turn your full attention on the other person for this process to be effective. The core of the meeting is to ask a *focusing question*: What are *your* goals? Third, you must use the information in a helpful way to provide feedback. Let's take these stages one at a time.

Schedule the Meeting

This process is effective with a new hire or with people who have worked with you for a period of time. If you've not conducted a meeting like this in the past, the individual may be a bit skeptical at first. Therefore, when you request this meeting, you must declare your "helpful intent." That is, you must relate to the other person and help him or her relax. You may want to outline what you would like to achieve at this meeting.

As an example: "Ralph, you've been with us for almost a year now. You know, we've never sat down and talked for any period of time. I'd like to get to know you better so I can help you reach your goals. Can we go to lunch sometime this week? I'd really like to get to know more about Ralph. Is Thursday good for you?"

If this is done in a genuine manner, the individual will look forward to the lunch.

During the Meeting

If you really don't know this individual very well, you need to engage in preliminary conversation that will give you insights into him or her as an individual. You may want to ask where they live and grew up, why they chose to attend their university, what activities they are involved in away from work, etc.

Once you complete the preliminaries, you need to restate your helpful intent. You may want to say something like, "Ralph, as I said on Monday, I'd like to get to know you better. If I can better understand your goals, I can do a better job of contributing to your reaching those goals."

Once you've established your helpful intent, you need to identify the individual's goals. You do this by asking a focusing question—a question in which you focus on a specific theme or subject. In this case, you are focusing on the goals. For example: "I know your job description and your performance standards for the coming year, yet we've never talked about things above and beyond those elements. What are your goals here at our organization? In other words, what do you really want to achieve?"

This is essential to the *inner view*. If you don't know the other person's goals, you can't help them achieve those goals. By asking open-ended questions, you can gather information. You want to gather as much information as you can on the goals of this individual because you will use this information in later interactions.

After the Meeting Provide Feedback

Once you have gathered the information, you must use the information. This is the key to the *inner view* concept. You must provide feedback in order to help keep the person on track to attain their goals.

Suppose the individual states a desire to move into a managerial position within your organization. This is a worthwhile goal for this person, and it is attainable. They have the qualities necessary to move into a management position. You notice that they are engaged in activity that is moving them away from the goal. It could be tardiness, overly long lunch breaks or personal phone calls, missed deadlines, etc. However, it is not an offense that needs reprimanding. This situation calls for a correction in the behavior. This is your chance to use the information gained at the *inner view* to help the individual make adjustments to correct those negative activities.

For example, let's pretend that you and I are astronauts and we are headed toward the moon on the latest space exploration. About halfway to our goal, we hear from Houston Ground Control: "Hey, hello, attention. You are a bit off course. You are 3 percent off to the left, and if you continue in that direction, you will miss your goal."

You aren't going to grab the microphone and yell back, "Hey! Don't tell us how to do our jobs. We are fully trained astronauts, and we know what we are doing. In fact, Tom Hanks is going to play me in the next movie!" You aren't going to do that. You are going to grab the microphone and speak very plainly as you ask for specific directions.

"Is it 3 percent or 4 percent? Should we adjust to the left or to the right?" You are going to make those adjustments, and the last thing you'll say is, "Thank you!" You can now correct your course, and you will have the chance to hit your target.

The same is true for the individuals you manage or lead. If they truly are in pursuit of an advancement, they will appreciate your input, make the necessary changes, and even say thank you. However, if you have discussed what they need to do to advance, and then you observe that they are not following the game plan, it is your responsibility to find out why. Perhaps they are not taking advantage of the training courses your organization provides for employees. The involvement in these courses will tell other managers that they are putting forth the effort in an attempt to prepare for a management position. You notice this and bring it to their attention.

"Ralph, I notice that you are not enrolled in the course on reading financial statements for the nonfinancial manager. Didn't you say you needed that to move into a management position?" He may say, "Well, my goals have changed." Now, this is important. In order to contribute to this person's growth and development, you need to know if his goals have changed. You don't want to give feedback on something that is not important or not going to be valuable to him.

If this is the case, if the individual's goals have changed, you must return to the stage of the *inner view* process where you asked, "What are your goals?" It is certainly permissible for a person's goals to change. However, for you to assist in helping them reach those goals, you must identify them.

Well, there you have it. The *inner view* provides you with a method to identify a teammate's goals and assist in helping him or her reach those goals. It provides a starting point in knowing your staff as people and not as units of production. It provides you with a reason for giving feedback and intervening when your teammate is getting off track.

Will this technique work? Only if you do!

PERFORMANCE PRINCIPLES
---

1. Assumptions are the cornerstone for miscommunication.
2. Don't assume that people are units of production, wanting what you want. Ask—get the *inner view*.

18

Education to Overcome Management Paralysis

Only the educated are free.

Epictetus

AWARENESS

ASSUMPTIONS

ANALYSIS

ACTION

The third *A* in our Four-A Formula is *Analysis*. When I'm talking about analysis, I'm talking about education. There are three great immobilizers that keep you from succeeding and, as a matter of fact, keep all of us from accomplishing what we are capable of. The *only* way to overcome these immobilizers is through analysis and education. The immobilizers are *fear*, *doubt*, and *worry*. These are three negative uses of our imagination.

Let's take a closer look at this concept of FEAR—False Evidence Appearing Real. Using a piece of cloth and my finger, chances are good I could come into your town and rob your bank. I could use the piece of cloth as a handkerchief to cover my face. Then I could put my finger in my coat pocket, giving it the appearance of a gun when I point it at a person. If I aimed it at the teller and said, "Give me your money!" I can guarantee you their palms would get sweaty and their heart would beat faster. At that point, they would give me the money. All the evidence would be false, but because it would appear to be real, the teller would act as if it were real.

You might have read about the young Cuban who years ago hijacked a plane to Cuba with nothing but a bar of soap. He placed the soap in a shoebox, went up to the flight attendant, and said, "Hey, I've got a bomb in here." She said, "Ooooooohhhh, you need to see the pilot!" He went to see the pilot and said, "Hey, I've got a bomb in here and I'd like to go to Cuba." They went to Cuba. All the evidence was false, but because it *appeared* to be real, the pilot acted as if it were real.

A Challenge for You

I want to challenge you to write down your ten greatest fears, doubts, and worries. Now some of you might say, "But I have more than ten fears, doubts, and worries!" Relax, I said your ten *greatest* fears, doubts, and worries. If you have the courage to write them down, here is what you will find: Out of the ten items you listed, seven or eight will already have happened or cannot happen. Of the remaining items, you have absolutely no control over one or two of them. And you will find that only one or two items are within your control.

Question: Does it make sense to dissipate your energies over a long list of things you cannot control instead of focusing your energies on the one or two things you can effectively handle? Since the answer is obviously no, why do we fail to focus our energies on solvable problems? Answer: Because we are creatures of habit. We have an everyday routine that we are involved in, and if the routine is changed, it upsets us and can even spoil our whole day.

Unfortunately for our society, one of our most destructive habits is griping, complaining, and moaning. Or, as Bryan Flanagan says, "We become members of the moan, groan, and carry on club!" Do you realize that some people would rather complain than succeed? If that sounds absurd to you, prove me wrong. Try eliminating the complaining and see if it doesn't help you move toward success more quickly. We live in a society that is used to being negative more than positive. For example, as my speaker friend Don Hutson says, economists have predicted eighteen of the last two recessions! People find fault as if there were a reward for it! Too many people look for the worst and never pass up the chance to cut down or criticize others.

Negative Use of the Imagination

As a general rule, I board an airplane from two to ten times each week. Obviously, I know that from time to time there are airplane crashes, so I recognize there is danger for me when I get aboard that aircraft. But realistically there is even more danger for the airplane, because when airplanes come down faster than they go up, their trade-in value drops to virtually nothing. I mean, you just can't swap them at all!

Interestingly enough, however, though there is danger when the plane leaves the ground, there is even more danger if the plane remains *on* the ground. Engineers will quickly tell you that the plane will rust out sitting on the runway faster than it will wear out flying in the sky—which is what airplanes are built for. When a ship leaves the harbor, there is certainly danger involved because, from time to time, ships do sink. But there's even more danger if the ship stays in the harbor. Again, the experts tell us that if it stays at anchor in the harbor, a ship will collect barnacles and become unseaworthy faster than if it is sailing the high seas—which is why the ship was built in the first place.

If you rent out your home, you take a chance that the person you rent it to will damage it. In some cases, renters simply do not have pride of ownership and will not take as good care of your home as you would. However, my real estate friends assure me the house is in greater danger if you leave it empty. They tell me it will deteriorate faster standing empty than it will if someone is living in it, and besides, homes are built to be lived in.

Obviously, there is a certain amount of danger in doing anything, but in management there is generally even more danger in doing *nothing*. Humans and nature are exact opposites in at least one respect: *We deplete nature's resources by using them up. We deplete our human resources by not using them at all.*

Oliver Wendell Holmes was right when he said the great tragedy in America is not the destruction of our natural resources, though that tragedy is great. He said the truly great tragedy is the destruction of our human resources by our failure to fully utilize our abilities, which means most men and women go to their graves with their music still in them. This tragedy is compounded when those of us in leadership positions do not utilize our abilities to properly direct and inspire those in our sphere of influence to become all they are capable of becoming.

Our corporate purpose, our reason for being in business, is to help people recognize, develop, and use their abilities. One of the vehicles we use to accomplish this is the I CAN course I mentioned earlier. It has positively affected over three million students and thousands of teachers all over the United States and Canada.

Several years ago in Rockford, Illinois, a young woman named Marcie Lemaree was taking the I CAN class. I say "taking the class," but actually she literally had to be forced into the classroom, screaming and kicking. She was such a disruption that the teacher finally said, "Marcie, if you will go to the library and listen to the tapes that go along with the I CAN course, I won't turn you in to the principal." Well, that sounded a lot better than sitting in class, so she listened to the tapes, and as she listened, some things started to make sense to her. Gradually her attitude changed. Marcie became involved in her school; she became aware of why her attitude was so important; she analyzed and got instruction on how she could be more effective; she became a manager of the basketball team and lettered in girls' track. She also placed fourth out of seven on the rifle team.

Now that may not sound like a big deal to you, but when I share with you (as Paul Harvey would say) "the rest of the story," it might make a difference. Marcie is legally blind. She had difficulty telling darkness from light. When she fired the rifle for the rifle team, someone would say, "No, Marcie, you're a little low and to the left, you need to come up and to the right." Did Marcie have reason to fear, doubt, and worry? You bet she did! Did she overcome those fears, doubts, and worries? You bet she did! How? The same way you and I overcome our fears, doubts, and worries— through *analysis* and *education*! Needless to say, she changed her input, which dramatically changed her output.

Managing Motivation Education

Most management books spend some time looking at behavioral scientists' views of motivation, and this can be so technical that it is difficult to understand. My approach will seem to some an oversimplification, but as I have often said, some of the greatest truths in life are the simplest. For that reason, I generally speak and write at the seventh-grade, third-month level. I've also found that if I keep it at this level, even college professors will be able to keep up with me. But as my good friend Dr. Steve Franklin, who was a college professor at Emory University in Atlanta, Georgia, said, "The great truths in life are the simple ones. You don't need three moving parts or four syllables for something to be significant."

Steve pointed out to me that there are only three pure colors—but look at what Michelangelo did with those three colors! There are only seven musical notes, but look at what Chopin, Beethoven, and Vivaldi did with those seven notes. Lincoln's Gettysburg Address contained only 262 words, and 202 of them were one syllable. Think of the impact those simple, direct words have had on our society! I know many of our problems are complex, but I believe a simple (not simplistic), direct approach, worded in simple, understandable terms is the best and most effective way to get results.

A Top Performer with Real Education

After reading this much of *Top Performance*, it might not surprise you that when I think of one of the smartest and most educated people I have ever known, I think of a person with only a fifth-grade education—my mother.

I will never forget an incident that took place when I was a small boy in Yazoo City, Mississippi. Periodically I was given a chance to do a few odd jobs for an elderly couple who lived several blocks from us. They ran a small dairy and were probably in their late sixties or early seventies. The man was blind. We needed the extra money because finances were desperately tight in the '30s.

I have forgotten some of the details of the incident, but the bottom line is that something went astray. The woman berated me unmercifully and said I had not done what I had said I was going to do and therefore she was not going to pay me for the considerable amount of work I had done. When I went home in tears and told my mother I was not going to be paid for what I had done, she was understandably unhappy. However, my mother was the most loving, wise, and gentle person I've ever known (the epitome of a Top Performer and the symbol of all the positive management skills taught in this book). She also had great faith and was most supportive and loyal. When I finished my story, she calmly took off her apron and said, "Let's go and talk with them, son."

My mother was a small woman. She was nearly fifty years old, and all the years of her hard work had taken their toll. When we approached the couple, the woman proceeded to tell my mother in no uncertain terms that I had not done what she'd expected me to do, that I was not dependable, that I had lied to her, and a number of other things. My mother, as all good managers do, patiently heard her out, listening very, very carefully and quietly until the woman finally finished.

Then my mother said, "Well, let me remind you that I was present when you hired my son to do this work. I remember exactly what you told him you wanted him to do in your yard. Before I knocked on the door, I made it a point to get a good look at your yard. I can tell you that not only has my son done everything you hired him to do, but in my opinion he has done a really good job and thrown in some extras as well. My son did not lie to you about this, and I want you to know that my son would never lie to you on any occasion about anything." Then my mother summed it up: "You owe my son the money, but whether you pay him or not is entirely up to you. I just wanted to make it very clear to you that my son is honest. If you don't pay him for what he has done, we will be able to live without the money, but are you going to be able to live with the money and the knowledge that you've unjustly accused my son of a wrong that he did not do? I leave it up to you as to whether you're going to pay him."

As nearly as I can recall, the woman was still adamant that I had not done what she had hired me to do, and my mother closed the conversation by saying, "That's all right. We can get along without the money. You just let your conscience be your guide."

A few days later the woman stopped by the house with the money and apologized to both my mother and me.

That was a particularly significant event in my life because my mother had stood by me, and though it was many, many years ago, I will never forget how grateful I was for the support she gave me. I believe incidents like this made a dramatic difference in my life. As managers and leaders, the support we give to our people when they are right is extremely important, and even when they are wrong, we can defend their integrity while not agreeing with some of their actions.

Two of my mother's favorite sayings were, "It's not *who's* right, but *what's* right," and, "If you've got the right person, what they're going to be doing is going to be right." Yes, my mother was a magna cum laude graduate of the school of life. If you will use the principles we are discussing in *Top Performance*, which she role-modeled so effectively, then you, too, will be recognized as a manager who helps employees overcome fear, doubt, and worry, and one who gets Top Performance from your people!

PERFORMANCE PRINCIPLES

1. Without the proper education, fear, doubt, and worry will immobilize you and your associates.
2. Once a need is satisfied, it is no longer a motivator. Satisfaction does not increase motivation.
3. Management Assumptions + Management Attitudes = Management Behavior

19

The Secret
to Management Motivation

Action often precedes the feeling.

Anonymous

AWARENESS

ASSUMPTIONS

ANALYSIS

ACTION

The fourth *A* in our Four-A Formula is *Action*! You are a person of action. It started this morning. You were lying in bed and that "opportunity" clock (negative folks call it an alarm clock!) went off. You reached over and shut it off, and in the process that cool air hit your elbow. And then you did what comes naturally—you quickly pulled your elbow back under the covers! Then you had a very basic decision to make: "Am I going to put *all* of me out there in that cold air, or am I going to keep *all* of me right here under these nice warm covers where I belong?" Because you are a responsible person with all the success characteristics we discussed in the first part of this book, the battle between *what you want to do* and *what you are committed to do* is won by *what you are committed to do*, and you roll out of bed. It's obvious to you and to every other success-oriented person that nothing happens until you take that first step—nothing happens until you get the action habit.

I want to share with you one phrase that I honestly believe is worth the price of this book. Now, just in case you're thinking, *Well, why didn't you put it on the first page and leave the rest out?* the answer is, "I don't want you to just get your money's worth. I want you to get a bargain." The reason is partly benevolent and partly selfish. As stated earlier, I firmly believe that you can have everything in life you want if you will just help enough other people get what they want. So why do I want you to get so much from this book? Answer: The more you get, the more people you will tell about the book, which simply means the sale of more books. Now here's that powerfully magic statement:

Logic will not change an emotion, but *action* will!

Or, phrased another way:

Action often precedes the feeling!

For example, I hate to be the one to break the news to you, but there are going to be days when you won't want to get out of bed and go to work. I know it will surprise some of you, but there really are going to be those days. However, sometimes the best work is done by people who don't want to do the things they have to do, but they have the old-fashioned guts, gumption, and sense of responsibility to get up and go! Who are the successful people? They are the people who do the things unsuccessful people refuse to do! They understand that every task they handle is a self-portrait of the person who performed it, and they have committed themselves to autograph every job with excellence.

As I stated in my book *See You at the Top*, one year I finished second in a national organization that employed over seven thousand salespeople. Later I finished first in another national organization that had over three thousand people in sales. I can state without reservation that there were many days when I did not feel like going to work, but I actually started to feel like working after I got into action. Here is a key point: Not once in that year when I was number two of seven thousand did I finish in the top twenty in sales for a single week. Not once in that time did I finish in the top twenty for a single month. Yet at the end of the year I was second in the organization. How did this happen? Simple! I disciplined myself to start *every* day by being in front of a prospect by no later than 9:00 a.m. The net result was *some* business *every* week, so that by the end of the year the cumulative total was enough to put me in second place.

As you well know, big jobs are accomplished by taking lots of small steps. How do you eat an elephant? One bite at a time! How do you lose thirty-seven pounds? By losing 1.9 ounces every day for ten months. How do you effectively lead your people to greater accomplishments and move steadily up the ladder of success? By steadily, on a daily basis, giving your job a "best effort." The only way to coast is downhill, isn't it?

You've Heard It Before—Take One Step at a Time

My sister-in-law, Eurie Abernathy, had multiple sclerosis (MS) for many years. In 1985 she spent several days with us over the Christmas holidays. It was her first visit in our new two-story home. Because of the MS, I assumed she could not make it up the stairs to the second floor, so I was surprised when I returned home one day and found her and the Redhead seated in our bedroom enjoying a chat. After a few minutes, Eurie decided to go back downstairs. As a precaution, I walked in front of her so that if she started to fall I could catch her.

As we made our way downstairs, I expressed surprise that she had been able to go up the stairs, which were relatively steep. She quickly responded with a simple but profound statement: "Yes, I can do anything I want to do, as long as I take it one step at a time." The opportunity for greatness, according to the late sales trainer Charlie Cullen, does not come cascading down like Niagara Falls. Rather, it comes slowly, one drop at a time!

Here is your challenge: Make a list of your ten most important action steps to success. Not what someone else must do to succeed, not what someone else thinks you should do to succeed, but what *you know you must do every day*! I fully understand that you do more than ten things daily, but what are the ten most important activities that translate to success for you?

Ten Action Steps to Success

1. _____
2. _____
3. _____
4. _____
5. _____
6. _____
7. _____
8. _____
9. _____
10. _____

At the time I set the sales records I spoke of, I was selling cookware. I was conducting demonstration parties, cooking with the heavy-duty, waterless cookware I was encouraging people to buy. Many times it would be midnight before the kitchen was cleaned and everyone was gone, but number one on my list was to be face-to-face with a prospect at 9:00 a.m. the next day. Regardless of the fact that the baby kept us up until 3:30 a.m.; despite the fact that the car had a flat tire or wouldn't start; regardless of any excuses, I was to be face-to-face with a live prospect at 9:00 a.m. *every morning*! When we set our goals and break them into bite-size pieces, there is no limit to what will be accomplished. A commitment to *start* each day at the same time and in the same way is really a commitment to finish, because starting is obviously the first step in arriving. Lawyer Adlai Stevenson was right: A journey of a thousand leagues begins with a single step.

What's Holding You Back?

It is an established fact that the largest and most powerful locomotive in the world can be held in place by a one-inch block of wood. Placed in front of the eight drive wheels of the locomotive, the block will hold it completely motionless. Yet that same locomotive, with a full head of steam, can crash through a steel-reinforced concrete wall that is five feet thick. That is what getting the action habit can do for us! This next example by William Moulton Marston is from the world of sports, but it certainly applies to us in the world of business.

Hitting the Ball

I asked Babe Ruth what was the most exciting moment of his career, and he told me it was during the third game of his last World Series in Chicago. He was in a batting slump, his team was behind, and two strikes had been called on him. The crowd turned against the Babe and began to boo. Ruth's desire to win rose to meet this emergency and he flashed into action. He pointed to a distant spot in the outfield and yelled back at the howling fans, "I'll knock it out there for you!"

Babe smashed the next ball to that precise spot. It was a home run, the longest hit ever made in Wrigley Field. I asked him what he thought about when the ball was pitched.

"What'd I think about?" he snorted. "Why, what I always think about—just hittin' the ball!"

There's your champion—the person who keeps their attention riveted on their present act and who responds positively to every crisis or desire with all there is in them. With the outcome of a World Series and his own contract for next year hanging in the balance, Ruth thought about hitting the ball. And because he wanted to win more than he ever had before, he hit the ball hard.

The next time you find yourself in a jam, with a string of mistakes behind you and everything hanging on your next move, forget both past and future. Remember Babe Ruth and think about just one thing—hitting the ball.

Let yourself go—give everything you have to your desire to win before the crisis passes. It will be the best performance you ever produced because of the emotional steam behind it. Every crisis offers you extra desired power.

Personal Conviction: Positive Thinking and Positive Believing

When we talk about being people of action, we recognize that action takes courage. Gerhard Gschwandtner of Fredericksburg, Virginia, started an excellent sales publication called *Selling Power*, which I highly recommend. One of my favorite parts of Gerhard's format is the interview with action-oriented people. In one issue, Mo Siegel was the interviewee. Mo Siegel is the founder and former owner of Celestial Seasonings, the herbal tea company that captured a major portion of the multimillion-dollar tea industry. He based his organization on a value system he equates with the four legs on a stool. The first leg is *love of product*. Mo Siegel surrounded himself with people who really loved herbal tea and believed it to be valuable to the consumer. The second leg of the stool was *love of customer* (which, in the case of Celestial Seasonings, was distributors). Celestial Seasonings put the customer first in quality-control decisions. The third leg of the stool was *love of art and beauty*, which led Mo Siegel to develop one of the most detailed (and expensive) packaging programs in retail sales. The fourth leg of the stool was *dignity of the individual*. Celestial Seasonings treated everyone (including employees) with the dignity every human being deserves. Any time a serious question arose within the organization, Mo Siegel said the solution would lie within the answers to two more questions: (1) Is the customer happy? and (2) Are we making the best possible product?

The answer to that second question led him to commission blind taste tests in which his product consistently beat the major black teas or nonherbal teas that have the major share of the market. Despite overwhelming evidence that Celestial Seasonings had a superior product, Mo Siegel refused to use the concept in an advertising campaign. His personal convictions led him to spend his time and resources in serving the customer better. He stated, "I decided I did not want to make a fortune by bad-mouthing anybody."

With the current trend in advertising doing exactly that, Mo Siegel's decision required courage and integrity. Siegel went on to say that "an organization values what it dedicates its time and resources to." In his case it is obvious that he values integrity. He also stated that the reason he was able to grow so big so quickly was his commitment to training. He said that managers need a minimum of thirty hours of training per year, and salespeople need even more. I might add that I agree with him that training is tremendously important, because it helps change a person from a "positive thinker" to a "positive believer."

Here's the difference: Positive thinking is the optimistic hope—not necessarily based on any facts—that you can move mountains or accomplish other seemingly impossible tasks. I've seen positive thinking and positive thinkers accomplish some incredible things. I've also seen some people get into serious trouble because all they had was positive thinking and enthusiasm. They had no foundations, no skills, no training. Consequently, they let their enthusiasm carry them away, and they ended up in serious difficulties. (Someone has said that positive thinking and enthusiasm are like running in the dark—it might get you there, but you might get killed along the way!) Add training to that positive thinking and enthusiasm and you turn on the lights for your trip to the top—which means you will arrive alive.

Positive believing is the same optimistic hope as positive thinking, but it is based on solid reasons for believing you can move mountains or accomplish other seemingly impossible tasks. I've seen positive believers accomplish far more than positive thinkers. Positive believers have even more enthusiasm than positive thinkers, even when things are not going well at the moment.

A good training program—which is obviously what Mo Siegel was talking about—gives the members of an organization solid reasons for believing they can accomplish much with their lives. They believe in their company, they believe in their product, and training enables them to believe in their ability to communicate that belief to others who will, in turn, take action by buying.

Positive thinking is always important, and it certainly will enable you to accomplish more than negative thinking will—but positive believing will enable you to do infinitely more than just positive thinking will. That's why in *Top Performance* we give so many steps, procedures, and actions to follow so that, as a leader and as a manager, you move more and more into the positive-believing realm.

Organizational charts help make positive believers out of positive thinkers. Once again Krish Dhanam has made what could have been dry reading interesting and extremely informational. Let's hear Krish's thoughts on this.

Teamwork and Process Improvement

A typical organizational chart (Figure A) shows that most organizations have processes that are designed so that customers end up supporting the entire organization. This includes both the internal and external customers in an organization. Top Performing organizations have found ways to invert this structure as shown in Figure B.

Figure A

Teamwork and *process improvement* are the two pillars upon which an inverted organization can stand. When an organization decides that its primary reason for existence is the service of both its internal and external customers, it is ready to support itself on the pillars of *teamwork* and *process improvement*.

The Organization of the Future

Figure B

Teamwork

The strength of a team can be impacted at any stage by anyone who has a positive or a negative influence on the outcome of the team's goals. Traditional teams have mandated performance by arbitrary standards that depend more on an organization's belief in what the individual is capable of doing than an assessment of capabilities of each member of the team. This leads to a belief that a work group is actually a team. In a bowling league, if one person bowls 300 and the others are just spares (for the pun of it)—the 300 bowler can carry the team. This is not a team. This is a work group where one performer is the workhorse with the tautest harness on his or her shoulders, and the rest of the players just go along for the ride. To create a foundation of Top Performers on your team, it is important to make sure they know they each are vital pillars in the organization.

Mr. Ziglar always makes sure his staff knows how vital they are. The following point he makes about teamwork is an excellent example of how he goes about it:

Top Performers in leadership/management positions recognize they have teams within teams. For example, the people with whom I work most closely are my wife, my executive assistant, and my youngest daughter, who is the editor of my books and newspaper columns. The three of them work beautifully together, love and respect each other, and definitely make my efficiency and effectiveness much greater. The burden they relieve from my shoulders is incredible.

Every team member in our company is important, and each one does a better-than-good job. However, just as in football, we have "special teams" like the kicking team, the defensive team, the offensive team, etc. Those special teams make a big difference. I believe everyone in our company is a difference maker, but the three who work the closest to me make the biggest difference in my own personal performance.

I suspect that most leaders/managers have their own special teams and, biblically speaking, Moses, David, and even Christ had their special teams.

Values

Sam Walton was a legend in his own time. He shared his values of simplicity and hard work until his very end. This created a culture of values-based performance within an entire organization. People did not feel that they worked for a discount store; they *performed* with the belief that they were change agents. The greeter's values were allowed to coexist with the manager's values, and the result was the largest corporation in the world, with gross revenues in excess of $59 billion.

Vision

The belief that one person can do something great is a myth.

John Maxwell

Vision is one of the greatest treasures that a person can hold. In most organizations, within the confines of everyday productivity, an individual's vision is not allowed to thrive alongside an organization's vision. Most performers in a team are always told about the collective end that is the goal of the team, the key point being they are never asked their opinion as it relates to the organization's vision. The constant painting of the big picture is important so that the individual performers will know that the people they follow do have a plan and a goal. However, not stopping to find out the individual vision of the contributing team players will make the pillars weak. If any person has to constantly search for their identity and dreams, that person's effectiveness to the cause entrusted to them is weakened. Successful leaders ensure Top Performance in their people by encouraging the individual vision and mission of each person on the team.

In 1994 Bryan Flanagan and I were in the Philippines conducting some training seminars. I reminded Bryan of how lucky I was to be enjoying the good life and then thanked him for believing in me when I was just a rookie salesman. Bryan told me that he believed in my potential contribution to the Ziglar team, and hence he did what he did. Believing in someone else's vision will go a long way toward ensuring their effectiveness to your team. We have since done a lot of things together, but

I will always be indebted to Bryan for his belief in me. At that point in my life, his belief in me was far greater than the belief I had in myself. Bryan is a Top Performer because his vision for the team was very clear and precise.

Victories

No one of us is more important than the rest of us.

Ray Kroc

No team can ever be successful if the individual victories are not celebrated. The most important acknowledgment a team player can get is that they are valuable to the team and winning without them would be impossible. Recognition was discussed at great length in chapter 11, so here we will deal with the need for every team member to know that he or she is a part of an organization's victory list. By putting victories under the belt of the team player at periodic intervals, you strengthen their contribution to the organization. This is more than an "atta boy" or a "well done," but it does not have to be monetary. It is sincere praise for their work. Many people leave an organization because they are not allowed to be a part of the celebration.

Process Improvement

Dr. W. Edwards Deming, who is considered the father of the quality movement that swept global enterprises in the late '80s and through the '90s, once remarked that a good percentage of all productivity problems is due to systems problems. An inverted organization designed to enhance the value provided to its internal and external customers in most cases comes up short because of systemic deficiencies in the processes that are in place. Systems issues tend to be chronic in nature. A *chronic problem* is defined as one that just won't go away. It is deep-seated in the system and has been there a long time. Management that operates without awareness of the situation tends to dislike chronic problems because they feel there is nothing they can do to solve them.

Sometimes managers and leaders who don't focus on process improvement prefer *acute problems* to chronic problems. Acute problems are short-term flare-ups that can be made to go away with the Band-Aid approach, but they will return because the solution treated the symptom and not the cause. Top Performing organizations focus on having constant process improvements that address both the chronic problems and the acute problems. Process improvement is an important ingredient because it ensures that effectiveness is maintained through the rank and file.

A simple motto to follow to ensure that all processes are considered important to an organization's financial health is:

1. Do the right thing.
2. Do it right the first time.
3. Do it right now.
4. Do it at the right price.

But every company claims to be doing these four things. In order to establish yourself as an organization that is a Top Performer, you need to add these six additional criteria to your system to give you the value edge in today's marketplace.

1. *Identify* what's important to your internal and external customers.
   a. Ask your internal customers how you can improve.
   b. Ask your external customers what they want through focus group methodologies.
2. *Take time* out of your schedule to really understand the components of every process in your organization. The consulting firm of Rath and Strong estimates that only 1 percent of the total process time is spent on steps that are important to the customer.
3. *Assign the cost component* or value of each of the steps of a given process to an organization's bottom line. Fortunately, studies have suggested that as much as 75 percent of the lost time can be reclaimed.

4. *Mandate* the need for and the importance of internal process management champions. Experience has shown that at least 75 percent of the steps making up any process are not beneficial from the customer's perspective. As such they are costly steps and need to be reduced or eliminated.

5. *Reduce* or eliminate unnecessary steps and processes.

6. *Serve* your customer's customer.

What do you suppose would happen to your market share if you were able to take 10 percent of your customers and provide your organization's products and services so well, so seamlessly, in such a synchronized manner, that your customer's customers clamored to do business with you? If you were able to engineer this, would your company's stock go through the roof? Would your own personal performance and productivity get noticed for the innovation you showed in eliminating unnecessary steps? The simplest thing any manager or leader can do is to identify which steps are important to an organization. Get rid of those that are the cause of both the acute and the chronic problems.

"Have You Joined the Team?"

Most of us work in departments as part of a network of people who make up our company's team. If our company's service or product is good, there are others to share the credit. If it's poor, there are people to share the blame. But if we believe the old saying that a chain is only as strong as its weakest link, we know that our company's performance is only as good as ours.

Each of us makes a choice as to the role we'll play on the team. Either we join it as an actively caring member, or we go through the motions from the sidelines. When we choose to join the team, we have a better, surer shot at work that brings us satisfaction. The choice is ours. Here are the key attitudes that take us off the sidelines.

I make a difference here. I know that what I do makes it possible for my office to run smoothly. The effort I put into my job shows up in the quality of my office's services and in my company's earnings.

I'm a part of what outsiders see when they judge my organization. With every letter, every phone conversation, every personal contact, I make a statement about the caliber of service we offer. In the course of a year, I make hundreds of valuable business contacts for us.

How I feel on a given day affects the people I work with. I help to set the tone here. I know that when I bring real enthusiasm to the job, I make a contribution few others can equal.

I take responsibility for what bothers me. When a situation is causing me trouble at work, I approach it as my problem. Whether it's a procedure that isn't working, a practice I feel is unfair, or a person I'm having difficulty working with, I do what I can to change the situation. Sometimes it takes patience. More often than not, it takes knowing when to speak up and when to wait and how to coolly and rationally use my powers of persuasion.

> Top Performers anticipate change and embrace the opportunity to change.

When I can't get a situation changed, I look for ways to minimize its effect on me. Most important, I remember that I've chosen to work here, and so long as I'm here, I'll give my best.

I take an interest in my company. I know that an organization is greater than the sum of its parts; it has a life and personality of its own. I'm interested in how this company got to be what it is today and how the people in it have grown as they have.

My knowledge of the workings of the company not only helps me in my work but also makes the work more interesting. It's part of what makes me a valuable employee here, and it helps me set my own career goals and plan my future.

I try to see the big picture—to think beyond my particular job to the kind of product or service I'd like to receive as a customer or client. Because I'm interested in what makes us successful, I notice what's happening in business, politics, or technology that's going to affect us.

I'm proud to be a strong, reliable member of my company's team. I know that my success, as well as my company's, depends on it.[1]

Take a few minutes each day to remind yourself of the positive affirmations listed above. And keep reading; Krish has more information on what it takes to be a Top Performer.

What Makes a Top Performer?

The timid performers in this world are threatened by change. The aggressive are comfortable, but the Top Performers in this world look at change as an opportunity. They understand that all meaningful change to combat the external forces comes from within. Top Performers understand that no one except a baby in wet diapers really welcomes change. Change is difficult, but Top Performers make excellence a habit to combat the tides of societal and organizational change. Just as knowledge "out of order" creates chaos, knowledge "in order" creates and formulates the expertise necessary to survive change. The ways that Top Performers get knowledge "in order" include:

1. Understanding Why You Work

Every day, Top Performers remind themselves of the reason behind their decision to work. It is relatively easy to get caught up in the negative ramblings of a mediocre society's below-average expectations. However, clarifying one's thought process to arrive at the primary motivation behind the choices we make is paramount for us to enjoy the choice. I remember when several years ago I hit the wall. My work was demanding time away from home, and the travel intensified. I came to a point of acute misery when I realized that my motives were not in tune with my understanding of what I did. Like most people at that time, I would announce to my family that what I did, I did for them. This forced me to work harder each time to provide for them.

I was earning money to pay the bills of guilt that my travels were costing. When I changed my vocabulary, my understanding changed and the job became easier. I now tell my family that what I do I am able to do because of them. It is because of the power and energy derived from their place in my life that I am able to function. Now home is my well of knowledge, where I must return after each trip to quench my thirst. The guilt has gone, and in its place I have an inner peace that validates my role, responsibility, dignity, sacrifice, and pride.

2. Working with Unconditional Loyalty

Several years ago, I suffered some embarrassment because a project that I was responsible for came up short on returns. There was a lot of dissent among my superiors, and their actions toward me were difficult at that moment in my life. I was on the receiving end of a stiff reprimand and did contemplate some retribution of my own. But cooler heads prevailed, and I called my father in India for his advice. He reminded me that human beings are prone to mistakes, and accepting responsibility for those mistakes is the right thing to do. However, he then asked me if I had been disloyal at any point. I replied that I had always been loyal and had never bad-mouthed my organization. He then told me that he was prouder of me because of that than any accolade I had ever received. In retrospect, it is the dignity that was shown through unconditional loyalty that allowed me to survive that rough period in my career. Zig Ziglar himself told me that my attitude toward the company during a time of adversity said more about my work ethic than any of the other contributions I had made.

3. Doing More Than You Are Asked to Do

America as a country has moved toward becoming a country of rights and gravitated slowly away from being a society of responsibility. One of the strange rituals practiced every day all across this country is the debate between the people who have to do the job and those who set the expectations. The popular belief is that we all are overworked and underpaid. This leads to a mind-set that says, "If you want me to excel, you have to pay me more." Organization leaders lodge a daily protest about the ineptitude of their workers. "Why can't these people do more than they are asked to? Don't they realize that people who perform without reward are the ones who will finish first?" It is a proven testimony from those who have excelled in their professional careers that a good work ethic guarantees your stability, whereas a poor work ethic assures your mediocrity.

The story is told about Mahatma Gandhi's letter to the inmates of the prison where he was being held captive. Amid the turmoil of the movement and the punishment he was receiving for his supposed treason against the imperial armies of the queen, he found time to do more. He wrote to the inmates about the benefits of staying healthy and the ways in which these benefits could be derived.

How many people do we know who think of doing more than they are asked to do and definitely more than they are paid to do? Going the extra mile is becoming obsolete as we have embraced the notion that doing something for the joy of others is not beneficial. Contrary to this belief, helping others and doing more than you are paid to do will get you abundance.

4. Be Patient and You Will Be Rewarded

Early in my career with the Zig Ziglar Corporation, I often complained about the time that it took to accomplish the smallest of victories. Bryan Flanagan reminded me that most people come up short because they expect the end of the process while still in the middle of the process. So true! The adage that Rome was not built in a day is one that gives us the formula for sustained excellence. In the long run, those who pace themselves with patience are the ones who will stand in the victory lane to receive the winner's laurel.

5. The Corner Office Is Not Something You Deserve

The archaic notion that your physical place in an office is based on your deserving it is a mentality that will guarantee your failure. Many of my business colleagues constantly remind me of how they wish they had a corner office. My personal productivity is not tied into how many windows I have. That is a false prestige that convinces you that who you are is determined by where you sit.

6. Lifting Someone Up Causes You to Rise

The Ziglar Inc. philosophy is, "You can have everything in life you want if you will just help enough other people get what they want." This is a paraphrase of the Golden Rule, which has been expressed in many languages and has survived many cultural interpretations. In an increasingly competitive computerized generation, men and women have decided that selfishness is the only way to go because doing good lands you in trouble. It is no wonder that a good majority of those needing help do not ask for it, and those capable of giving it do not volunteer their assistance.

Action completes our Four-A Formula. Action brings *awareness* and *analysis* to fruition. It also does away with *assumptions*. Top Performance as a person or as a manager depends on all four.

If you will take action on the concepts Krish and I have talked about in this chapter and consciously make a decision to join the team, then you will become even more of a Top Performer.

PERFORMANCE PRINCIPLES

1. More people act their way into thinking than think their way into acting.
2. Logic won't change an emotion, but action will.
3. Action often precedes the feeling.
4. If the first three principles sound a great deal alike, congratulations! You are catching on!

20

It Takes Time

There can be no persevering industry without a deep sense
of the value of time.

Lydia H. Sigourney

The unfortunate truth is that far too many executives are so gung ho and
goal oriented from a career point of view that they often lose perspective and balance as far as their spiritual, personal, family, and social lives
are concerned. The primary reason for this chapter, which I consider the
most important one in the book, is to encourage you to become a Top
Performer in your spiritual, personal, family, and social life as well as in
your business career.

This excerpt from an article by Eugene Peterson in *Christianity Today*
puts the importance of the ability to relax in proper perspective:

In Herman Melville's *Moby Dick* there is a violent, turbulent scene in which
a whaleboat scuds across the frothing ocean in pursuit of the great white
whale, Moby Dick. The sailors are laboring fiercely, every muscle taut, all
attention and energy concentrated on the task. The cosmic conflict between
good and evil is joined: the chaotic sea and demonic sea monster versus the
morally outraged man, Captain Ahab.

In this boat there is one man who does nothing. He does not hold an oar; he does not perspire; he does not shout. He is languid in the crash and the cursing. This man is the harpooner, quiet and poised, waiting. And then this sentence: "To insure the greatest efficiency of the dart, the harpooners of this world must start to their feet out of idleness, and not from out of toil."

In the corporate world we may not be faced with physical danger or have a great need for a burst of physical energy, but we are faced with different kinds of "opportunities" that are emotionally and physically draining. To move into these challenges from a time of restful rejuvenation can make a significant difference in our effectiveness.

Take Time to Get Started

One of my favorite methods of doing this is to start the day—especially in cold weather—in my office at home with the gas logs burning. Sometimes I sit there quietly, thinking through a planned project or agenda, wrestling with the best and most creative way to handle an "opportunity," reading Scripture, or thinking on inspirational thoughts or messages. The first few minutes are the toughest. The temptation to get up and move around is sometimes overwhelming, but I can assure you that if you will quietly sit there, some very creative, inspiring thoughts and ideas will be yours by the time you rise.

You also can, without any notes, quietly work through some situations in which you've been involved. Maybe there's a problem or a puzzle you've been unable to solve. As you are sitting there (in most cases not totally awake), you're still in the "alpha" level of consciousness. At this level your creativity is at its very, very best—a marvelous, extremely productive way to start the day!

The second option you have for starting your day also involves getting up earlier. This option includes reading something of an inspirational na-ture, such as the Bible or an inspirational book, or listening to recordings that are motivational in nature. Reading and listening are both marvelous ways to get "up" for the day. As a matter of fact, some psychologists have determined that your first encounter of the day has a more direct bearing on your attitude for that day than your next five encounters. Now I'm not speaking about a "Hello" encounter; I'm talking about a significant encounter where you spend time with a person. With this in mind, if you set aside fifteen to thirty minutes early in the morning to "encounter" someone of your choice, either to listen to an inspirational recording or to dig into an inspirational book, you will have made a deliberate choice to start your day with someone who will lift you and inspire you. With that kind of start, it's much easier to keep the momentum going.

The third option for the day, and a very effective way to start it, is with exercise. Later in this chapter I will give you the reasons for an exercise program, but it is sufficient to say that one of the most exciting ways to start your day is with physical exercise of some kind. This can involve lifting weights, swimming, bicycle riding, walking, or jogging. At any rate, a good exercise program gets the adrenaline flowing and those endorphins hoppin', and you've gotten the day off to a flying start.

Yes, I'm absolutely convinced that when you start your day in one of these three ways, and then awaken the other members of the family, your prospects for a productive day are infinitely greater. Your mate will be especially appreciative, and you can enhance your family relationships if you awaken him or her with that steaming cup of coffee (or better yet, herbal tea) and a few minutes of getting reacquainted in the morning. Then casually and lovingly awaken the children, and while one team member prepares breakfast, the other one can help the kids get ready for school.

Since breakfast is such an important part of the day, both physically and emotionally, husband and wife (and children, if there are any) should sit down and have a nutritious breakfast together at a more leisurely pace. It properly starts the kids' day, the family's day, and your day on a high note. It will make an overall difference in your own attitude and your own physical well-being—not to mention what it will do for the kids and your mate. When time is set apart for a healthy breakfast, more harmony will develop in the family.

One thing that is becoming more and more obvious is that when there is harmony in the family, the effectiveness of the manager on the job is noticeably enhanced. As part of this concept, we know a good, nutritious breakfast enables a person to perform more efficiently and effectively during the day. Eating together establishes bonds between family members that simply cannot be established in any other way. These bonds are most effective. I say it again—take time to get started.

Take Time to Grow

We have emphasized throughout *Top Performance* the necessity of personal growth for maximum business success. We're all familiar with the story of the woodcutter whose production kept going down because he did not take time to sharpen his ax. As we've indicated throughout this book, the top companies, the ones with the exciting bottom lines, have training and personal growth as major corporate objectives. It's true, the companies "on the go" are also "on the grow." Individually *you* need to take time to grow.

There are many ways to do this, of course, but one of the most effective ways is listening to inspirational material in your car. There are literally thousands of hours of recorded material that can be enormously helpful to you while you're going to and from your work. You can learn everything from Chinese art to a foreign language. You can learn how to set goals or close sales. You can learn how to invest in real estate and save on your income tax.

As a matter of fact, a study done several years ago at the University of Southern California revealed that you can acquire the equivalent of two years of college education in just three years while you're going about your normal activities in your automobile. This is assuming you live in a metropolitan area and drive twelve thousand miles each year.

Think about it. By utilizing your time in your car, you can become knowledgeable—even an expert—in your chosen field and several related ones. That gives you incredible security, regardless of what happens to your company or your relationship with your company. The exciting thing is that to acquire knowledge in that method is one of the fastest, easiest, and certainly one of the most painless ways ever devised.

Second, you can grow through the utilization of the marvelous books that are available today. Bookstores carry an enormous assortment of books that deal with virtually any subject related to your career and specifically with any aspect of dealing with self and interpersonal relationships.

Needless to say, the public library also offers a variety of books if you do not feel inclined to buy them. It is my own personal conviction, however, that as a manager and as a leader, you need to build a substantial library of your own. Personally, I would hesitate to put a price tag on the dollar value of my library, but it would run into thousands of dollars.

Let me offer a few suggestions about how you should read and effectively use your books. First—and I realize this sounds selfish—I encourage you to be protective of your books. Keep them for your own personal use or permit others to use them only in your library. In most cases, I encourage you to say no to anyone who wants to borrow a book. (I know for a fact that people often don't return books. I have a number of books in my own library that I have no idea how they got there!) If someone cannot afford the book, then do one of two things: Encourage them to join the library or, if it's a friend, go ahead and buy the book for them. As you build your career and develop your leadership skills, you need to have the resources you accumulate at your fingertips. Most doctors and attorneys do not loan their resource material. Your needs are just as great, and your professionalism should certainly be equal to that of a doctor or lawyer.

When I read a book or *anything* else, I always have a pen in my hand and I profusely mark the parts that are important to me. I underline, circle, make notes, etc. In the front of the book I jot down page numbers of those things that are particularly important and significant and that I feel will be useful in the future. I then file the books in my library according to the categories of study. This way, when I need information on a particular subject, I go to the correct section, open the book, and find notations in the front directing me exactly where to find what I need.

Of all the skills I have acquired, I believe the ability to read and to enjoy reading is one of the most important things I've ever learned. I encourage you, as a leader, not only to teach your children how to read but also how to *enjoy* the reading—make it come alive for them and they will be better for having done it. Ditto for your associates and subordinates. As you read good books and listen to audio resources, you'll have a daily source of magnificent inspiration.

A third area of growth should be through meetings and seminars. There are many marvelous educational seminars around this country that can

216

help you to hone your skills and develop them to the degree that will enable you to move up the ladder of success and happiness much faster and more effectively. As a practical matter, you should set aside at least one full week each year to go to seminars and personal growth opportunities that enable you to develop and bring out your inherent abilities. You should also be open to attending half-day and full-day specialized seminars once or twice each month.

I say it again: To really make it big in life—in all areas of your life—you need to take time to grow. It's not a question of whether you do or do not have time. Obviously, you do not have that option. You don't have time *not* to grow.

Take Time to Be Healthy

One question I often ask my audiences is, if there is a person there who has a Thoroughbred horse worth an excess of a million dollars. So far, no one has raised a hand. I then ask the question, "If you did have a Thoroughbred worth a million dollars, would you keep him up half the night, letting him drink coffee or booze, smoke cigarettes, and eat junk food?"

At this everybody laughs, because they realize that not only do Thoroughbreds not drink coffee or alcohol or smoke cigarettes but the idea of jeopardizing the horse's health—which obviously destroys the performance of the animal—would be so ridiculous as to be beyond discussion.

Then I ask, "Suppose you had a ten-dollar dog? Would you treat him that way?" And again there is laughter. "What about a five-dollar cat?" Then I point out that most of us would not treat a five-dollar cat like we treat our own billion-dollar bodies. As far as a million-dollar Thoroughbred is concerned, if we had such an animal, we would probably keep him in an air-conditioned barn in the summertime and a steam-heated one in the wintertime. We'd hire the best veterinarian money could buy to look after him and bring in a special nutritionist to make certain he was properly fed. In addition to that, we would get the finest trainer available to develop his potential. You can count on it—we would take care of a million-dollar Thoroughbred, yet we abuse our own billion-dollar bodies.

Taking care of our bodies is a reasonably simple routine. I did not say "easy." There are several factors involved, and since I'm not an expert on any of them, I will simply make some observations and aim you at some of the experts. To begin with, I encourage you to pick up Dr. Kenneth Cooper's book *The Aerobics Program for Total Well-Being*. This deals not only with exercise but with proper nutrition as well.

One of the things you need to consider is the amount of sleep you get. Some people do quite well on four or five hours. In my own case, I've discovered that it requires seven and a half hours of sleep for me to achieve Top Performance. Since I know that, I conscientiously work at getting that amount of sleep each evening. I can get by one night with much less sleep and do fairly well after a second night, but if I go three nights in a row, I can guarantee you that I am at considerably less than my most effective best by the third day. For that reason, I work and concentrate on getting a reasonable amount of sleep.

Exercise is the second area that is extremely important. These days I am a walker—I literally *love* to walk. However, there are many people who do not like that particular exercise—or any other. According to Dr. Cooper, the important thing is that you keep your heartbeat up for at least twenty minutes on about four occasions each week. Fast walking is a marvelous exercise. Riding a stationary bicycle—or, for that matter, riding a bike in the streets—is excellent exercise. You might consider those mini-trampolines where you simply bounce up and down—they do a great job. Others prefer swimming, and some experts say that is the most beneficial of all exercise programs. Still others enjoy cross-country skiing or racquetball, tennis, etc. Intelligent adults always begin their exercise programs by seeing the doctor. Please *do not* skip this most important step.

I am often asked, "Well, Zig, with as much as you have to do, when do you have time to exercise? When do you have time to walk?" I often tell people that I've got so much to do, I don't have time *not* to exercise. Incidentally, when I'm on the road and the weather is bad, I walk up and down the corridors of the hotel or motel where I'm staying. On occasion I go into the hotel ballroom or meeting room and speed walk around it. On other occasions, I've walked in a shopping mall. I am not a hero and therefore do not walk on dark streets at night. If the weather is good but it's night and I'm not absolutely certain of the area, I simply walk in the parking lot or the parking garage of the facility at which I am staying.

Let me point out that when you jog or exercise, you activate the pituitary gland. The pituitary gland floods the system with endorphins, which are over two hundred times more powerful than morphine. The net result is that you are on a "natural chemical high" for two to as much as four or even five hours. I have found the best time investment ever to be my time invested in exercise. An hour invested in exercise (counting time to dress, exercise, shower, cool down, etc.) returns two to four times that much high productivity time. The ideal time, according to Dr. Cooper, is in the latter part of the afternoon or early evening. By exercising then, you actually extend your effective workday by several hours.

Number three, in order to be at your healthiest, I encourage you to eat a sensible diet. By that I mean a well-balanced diet, and again Dr. Cooper's book will be helpful. In my own diet I concentrate on fresh vegetables, fish, chicken, and whole-grain cereals, and I seek as much roughage as possible. In addition to that, though there is widespread disagreement on this subject, I have been taking a natural food supplement for a number of years. Many doctors will tell you that in a well-balanced diet you will get the minimum daily requirements for your health. My point, though, is simply that I am not interested in minimum daily requirements. I am interested in maximum daily performance, and for that reason I do use a natural food supplement.

The fourth step in caring for your health is to eliminate the negatives. Smoking is a tremendous negative. Nineteen deaths out of every one hundred are directly traced to the habit of smoking. As I mentioned earlier, each time you light a cigarette you take fourteen minutes off your life span. Needless to say, if you smoke cigarettes, you're not going to enjoy the maximum health that you could otherwise enjoy.

Alcohol is another one of those elements in your life that in most cases can be enormously destructive. If you are a "casual" drinker, I encourage you to read *Dying for a Drink* by Anderson Spickard and Barbara R. Thompson. It may put drinking in a different perspective. I don't pretend to be an authority on the subject, but I've seen a great deal of grief resulting from drinking, and I do know that one "casual, social drinker" out of nine will eventually end up with a serious drinking problem. I also know that alcohol is a depressant and that people don't function as effectively when they've had a drink as they do without that drink.

Obviously, the other poisons you want to eliminate are those harmful legal and illegal drugs. The evidence against marijuana, speed, cocaine, and heroin, as well as many other drugs, is overwhelming. I cannot believe anyone with the intellectual capacity to occupy a leadership or management position would be so foolish as to ignore the overwhelming evidence as to what these substances do to a person and then deliberately "play" with them on a casual basis.

Thus far in my own career, I have never met a single human being who deliberately set out to become an alcoholic or who deliberately had as an objective to become a "pothead" or a drug addict. The question you need to ask yourself is: Is it worth even a slight risk to experiment with these substances that can destroy me personally, socially, and professionally, and wreck my family all at the same time? When I'm talking about taking time to be healthy, I'm also talking about eliminating the poisons that some people choose to put into their systems.

Take Time to Play

Most of the gung ho businesspeople I know set goals of acquiring new cars, getting promotions, having a certain amount of money in the bank, living at a certain residence, acquiring some educational degree, achieving a plateau of accomplishment, or excelling in a certain area. They set goals in every area of their lives, but often they do not set their objectives properly when it comes to taking time to play. I am absolutely convinced that unless we schedule recreational activities for ourselves and for our families, our own mental, physical, social, and family relationships are going to suffer. When that happens, it's just a matter of time before our careers will suffer.

When you check on the top-level executives, you discover that one of the major problems is executive burnout. This problem can be at least partially alleviated with a willingness to take the time to play. It could be racquetball or tennis or a regularly scheduled round of golf. It could be joining the company slow-pitch softball team or playing pickup basketball.

My friend Dr. James Dobson, the Christian psychologist who has had such an effective ministry through his radio program and his publications, is one of the busiest men I've ever encountered. Yet he would consistently invest an hour each day in physical exercise.

I believe the capacity to relax and enjoy yourself is an absolute must for those who would climb the ladder and then maintain their position once they have achieved it. You bring a fresh perspective, a fresh excitement, a fresh enthusiasm to what you're doing when you are enjoying life itself. I don't mean just enjoying your job but also enjoying the fact that you are alive and well and that you are getting more out of life than a paycheck.

A move up the corporate ladder and recognition as a community leader can be, even *should* be, your objectives. Financial success and corporate ladder climbing are worthy objectives, but within themselves they do not make you happy if you're not having fun along the way. There is nothing wrong with scheduling your playtime just as enthusiastically as you schedule your work time. I'm assuming you understand that I'm not talking about playing as much as you work, but a regular game of handball or racquetball, a round of golf, or an evening with the family at the movies, theater, church, or community activity on a regular basis can make a difference in your quality of life as well as your accomplishments in life.

Take Time to Be Quiet

When I handle this subject in my speeches, I always prepare the audiences by saying, "My next statement is probably going to surprise you, because generally speaking I am quite outgoing." I'm so loud from the platform that you might not realize or think in terms of my being quiet, but actually I am by nature a quiet person. Regardless of our natures, *all* of us need to take time to be quiet.

As I indicated when I talked about taking time to get started, we do live in a busy and noisy world, and there are those occasions when your batteries are simply going to run down. When that happens, no amount of superficial charging is going to restore those energy cells to their proper level unless you take that time to be quiet. I dearly love to walk, and my favorite time to walk, particularly in the summer months, is in the evening under a bright, moonlit sky. It seems that when those conditions prevail and I'm walking in the neighborhood I love so much, I have a renewal of energy that is absolutely incredible. My most productive ideas frequently come during that walking time.

Another of my favorite quiet times is early in the morning when I get up and go into my office. During that period of time some of my most creative ideas are born.

I strongly encourage you to take time to be quiet. There are occasions when you will want to share that quiet time with someone you love—a slow walk (this is not for exercise purposes) with a son or daughter or your mate, when you are in no hurry to do anything except be with that person. It's amazing how close you can draw to that individual as you walk, but it also is amazing how you will develop ideas when you explore with someone you love in a casual, unhurried, completely relaxed manner a concept or idea you've been wrestling with. When talking in detail to your mate about your business, even though your mate may not have the expertise or specific knowledge you possess, you'll be astonished at how much he or she can contribute with fresh insights. Spouses are generally free of your job-related prejudices, and they're not encumbered with a lot of preconceived ideas, so they can look at the overall picture and come up with ideas that are meaningful and helpful. The questions they ask can provoke creative thinking on your part and perhaps force you to take a look from a different perspective.

I can't overemphasize that you must take time to be quiet. It may be a few minutes puttering around in your garden, pulling weeds, or looking at great length at some of the miracles of nature that are all around us for our enjoyment if we will but take time to take a peek. Need I remind you that it was during those still, quiet moments at Valley Forge that George Washington found the strength to deal with the problems of winning our freedom and looking after freezing, starving troops? Need I remind you that it was during those still, dark moments during that great Civil War that threatened to split our nation asunder that Abraham Lincoln found the strength and the resolve to pull our nation together and see to it that we were reunited as one? It was during those still, quiet moments at Gethsemane that Jesus Christ found the strength to face the awful ordeal that was in front of him. During still, quiet moments you will find resources that you might never have known existed. Take time to be quiet—and to listen.

Take Time for Those You Love

One tragic myth that permeates our society is the belief that you can't be a hard-charging, successful businessperson *and* a loving, caring spouse and parent. That myth was exploded several years ago and reinforced in a *U.S. News & World Report* article on the one million "ordinary" millionaires. This article pointed out that 80 percent of millionaires came from middle- or working-class families and that a stable home life with few outside distractions provided the ordinary millionaire with the stamina to persevere in business. Most of them had lasting marriages, often to their high school or college sweethearts, and they were likely to "spoil" (be especially kind to) their spouses and children. They often suffered adversity. Twice as many salespeople as doctors would be millionaires by age sixty, and less than 1 percent of the millionaires were artists, entertainers, writers, and athletes. To me, what this really says is that successful people—including successful managers—have a balanced approach to life. The next example emphasizes this point.

Several years ago I stopped by to congratulate the president of a major corporation on his recent promotion. He greeted me with considerable enthusiasm and insisted I sit down so he could share with me the role he said I had played in his promotion. This was entirely unexpected, since my sole purpose was to invest sixty seconds to express my congratulations, but the new president would have none of it.

"You know, Zig," he said, "I honestly believe your talk on courtship after marriage, which we use in our video training department, played a substantial role in this promotion." Then he went ahead and told me the story.

"Our marriage was one of those that was truly out of the book. We both came from the 'right side of the tracks,' both went to marvelous schools, both came from successful family backgrounds. Upon graduation from college, we got married, and I proceeded to join the 'right' clubs, while my wife started serving in the 'right' charities. We were active in our church and had the 'right' number of children." (Meaning they had two.

I'm glad my parents didn't feel that was the right number, since I was the tenth of twelve!)

He continued his story: "I want to emphasize, Zig, that our marriage was a good one, but over the years we had gotten a little platonic in our relationship. But as I listened to you talk about your Redhead, I realized that although I had nearly twenty fewer birthdays than you, there seemed to be more excitement in your marriage, so I determined to see if the same thing could happen in mine. I was particularly intrigued with the fact you pointed out that, according to a West German insurance company, when a man kissed his wife good-bye—really kissed her good-bye [not like his little sister, but as we'd say down home, really 'stropped one on 'er!'], those men lived 5.6 years longer than the men who neglected this pleasant little interlude in their lives on a daily basis. [Fellows, your life is at stake!] Not only that but these men earn from 20 to 30 percent more money than do the men who leave home without kissing their wives.

"With that in mind," he said, "I decided to start really courting my wife. I started picking up the phone and giving her a call for a moment or two during coffee breaks each day. I frequently dropped a little note in the mail or bought her a neat little card, or I would take a single flower home. On occasion we had those 'heavy dates' when we really went out for a marvelous time. I went back to opening all doors for her, standing up when she got up to leave the table, holding her chair when she returned—all the little things she so deeply appreciated. Now, Zig, I'll have to confess that the changes were not instantaneous, but in a matter of just a few weeks, excitement definitely returned to our marriage. The intriguing thing is that excitement carried over into the marketplace and made me a happier, more productive executive. I'm absolutely convinced my efforts at the company were recognized and I was promoted to the presidency primarily because of the increase in my effectiveness, which was brought about by the excitement that returned to my marriage. So I just want to say thank you."

I left his office and headed upstairs to congratulate the chairman of the board, whose promotion had created the presidential vacancy. The president called to tell him I was on my way. The chairman was equally enthusiastic and insisted I sit down, because he, too, had a story to tell. He pointed to the telephone on the back of his credenza and said, "You know,

Zig, for a long time when that phone rang I was tempted to snatch it off the hook and demand to know, 'What have the little monsters done now?' Yes, I'm embarrassed to say my teenage son and teenage daughter were little monsters who were driving me up the wall. It seemed that everything my son ate turned to hair, his room was an absolute disgrace, and his stereo could be heard three blocks away. He was totally void of motivation and, even though (or was it because?) I rode him constantly, nothing was getting done. His fourteen-year-old sister had to be one of the most disrespectful, sassy children anywhere. Frankly, I was at my wits' end, and I didn't realize it until later, but I was actually avoiding any kind of contact with them at this point in our lives.

"However," he said, "something you said in one of your talks really got my attention. You pointed out that, from time to time, all of us need to just close our eyes and visualize that everyone and everything we love was suddenly taken completely out of the picture. [I learned that from my friend and fellow speaker Herb True.] When that really hit me, it dawned on me that if something happened to either of my kids, I would be a broken-hearted man because, despite all of our communication difficulties, I deeply loved them.

"On impulse one afternoon, I picked up the phone, called my son, and asked him if he would like to go watch the Detroit Tigers play the Texas Rangers. When my son recovered from the shock, he said, 'Sure, Dad.' The next day I took off an hour early, picked up my son, and we arrived at the ballpark a solid hour before game time. We were able to get excellent seats behind first base and though we are not 'baseball fans' in the real sense, we really got into the act that evening. We quickly learned that we were to boo the other team and cheer the home team, that we would be wise to question the eyesight and integrity of the umpire, and that our guys were always right and the other guys were always wrong. We took the seventh-inning stretch, ate lots of peanuts, drank lots of pop, and ate hot dogs. When it was all over, we went out for a snack, and it was well past one o'clock when we returned home."

He said, "I actually spent more time with my boy that night than I had spent with him in the previous six months. I'm not going to tell you that everything was instantly better, but the walls did start crumbling—the communication barrier was broken. We started talking and building a relationship." With tears in his eyes he said, "You know, Zig, I relearned that not only is my son an unusually bright boy, but he is also of high moral character, and I'm convinced he's going to do something with his life. Strangely enough, I never said another word about his hair and yet today it is respectable in length. I never mentioned cleaning up his room and, to be honest, if the health inspector were to inspect, it would not qualify for a Grade A restaurant permit, but it is acceptable in our home. And as far as the stereo is concerned, we all now enjoy the fact that his music can be heard clearly and distinctly in his own room but not at the next-door-neighbor's house.

"Not only that, Zig, but a few days later I called my fourteen-year-old daughter and asked her if she'd like to go out to dinner with me that evening. She was delighted, and so I told her to put on her fanciest party dress because we were going to one of those really nice restaurants where I take my important corporate clients. That evening I picked up a little corsage, and she looked so pretty in her dress with that flower! We spent over three hours at dinner that evening. We ordered hors d'oeuvres, the fancy entrée, and topped it off with a flaming dessert. What a delightful time we had!

"It's almost the same story as with my son. The barriers came tumbling down. I learned that not only is she a very, very bright girl, but she has definite objectives in her life. I believe someday she's going to be a marvelous wife and a good mother if she decides to go the family route, or she's going to have an outstanding career in her chosen field if she decides to concentrate on a business career. More important, Zig, I can tell you that when I leave home every day, I know all I have to concentrate on is my job. I'm convinced I am currently the chairman of the board because of the fact that my family situation has straightened up so much. I can commit all my creative energy to my job when I'm on the job, because I know everything is fine on the home front."

Isn't it ironic that these two enormously successful corporate executives, who were spending countless hours on their jobs and, as they often told everybody else, "I'm doing this for my family," discovered that when they neglected their families, they were not nearly as effective in the corporate world? Once they got their family lives in balance, their corporate lives also improved. I'm convinced that regardless of whether you are an athlete or an entertainer, whether you're in business for yourself or work for a major corporation, if you pay attention to the fires on the home front and keep them burning properly, you will move up faster, more effectively, and far more happily in the corporate world.

Yeah—but Where Do I Get the Energy?

I have a feeling that virtually every reader will agree, at least in principle, with the idea that a good relationship with your family is helpful to your business career. However, you just might be thinking, *Yeah, but where do I get the energy to be a good family person* and *a super manager?* This next illustration should provide you with at least a partial answer.

All of us are motivated by somebody or something in our lives. That's important to understand because motivation literally creates energy. As a matter of fact, in most cases when we claim to be "tired," we are actually mentally or emotionally drained and not physically exhausted. In short, our motivational bucket is running low. For example, have you ever had "one of those days"? You started with a flat tire that caused you to miss an important engagement. Your office manager called in sick and you had to handle an incredible number of administrative details, which you intensely dislike. The air-conditioning unit malfunctioned and made an already boring meeting an impossible one. On top of that, your most productive supervisor resigned. I mean *nothing* went right, and on top of that there was some evidence that you were developing a summer cold. Finally, however, the day mercifully ended and at 5:00 p.m. *sharp* you wearily headed home for some much-needed collapsing time.

Your smiling, enthusiastic spouse cheerfully welcomed you home and expressed delight that you did not have to work late because "today is the day." With some dismay you inquired, "The day for what?" Your spouse responded, "Why, honey, you remember. Today is the day we've planned for three weeks. Today we're going to clean the garage." Your reaction lay somewhere between exhaustion and anger as you protested that after the trials and tribulations of the day, you couldn't even pick one foot up— much less the four thousand boxes you needed to move to clean the garage!

227

Undaunted, your helpmate assured you that the two of you would work together and it would take only three or four hours.

At that moment the phone rings and, with a tremendous burst of energy, you manage to lift the receiver all the way to your ear and say hello with all the enthusiasm of a kamikaze pilot on their thirty-third mission. The voice on the other end is that of your best golfing buddy with the good news that they have a tee time at the country club in just twenty-three minutes if you feel like getting in a fast nine holes before dark. Guess what? That utterly exhausted, can't-take-another-step body of yours suddenly explodes with energy! The formerly lifeless legs propel you out to the garage—not to clean it but to grab those golf clubs and hurry out to the country club. You are *motivated*!

Now I'm not about to suggest that your golfing buddy is a better motivator than your spouse, but the energy-building motivational appeal (hitting golf balls) was substantially more to your liking than was your spouse's inducement ("killing" yourself cleaning that garage!). Your friend was being an effective manager by *channeling the energies* you had in a direction you wanted to go.

Effective people managers channel their own energy, as well as the energies their people possess, at a target they want and need to reach. You've learned how in *Top Performance*. Now do it.

PERFORMANCE PRINCIPLES ———

1. Take time to get started.
2. Take time to grow.
3. Take time to be healthy.
4. Take time to play.
5. Take time to be quiet.
6. Take time for those you love.

EPILOGUE

A Unique Opportunity

When I was a small boy in Yazoo City, Mississippi, I worked in a grocery store. Now you must understand that in the late '30s and early '40s, things were dramatically different from what they are today. At that time very few kids had money to buy sweets. Molasses candy was one of the delicacies of the day. People would buy molasses and make candy from it. The molasses was kept in a big barrel at the store. When customers brought their jars or jugs in for molasses, we simply filled them from that huge barrel. From time to time one of the little guys in town who had nothing to do would come into our store to kill time and hope for a handout.

One day he was in the store, and when he thought no one was looking, he carefully took the top off the molasses barrel, stuck his finger in, and put it in his mouth. As he was licking his lips, my boss suddenly appeared and grabbed him by the shoulders, shook him, and said, "Son, don't you ever do that again! That's not sanitary and we won't stand for it!"

The boy was somewhat shaken, but as he left the store I could tell he was going to survive. A few days later he showed up in the store again. He walked around a few minutes, carefully looked, and when he did not see the owner, he removed the top of the barrel and ran his finger through the molasses. Just as he popped his finger into his mouth, suddenly out of nowhere my boss appeared. This time he swatted the little guy across the rear a couple of times and told him to get out of the store and never come back.

You would have thought the kid had learned his lesson, but about ten days later that sweet tooth obviously had gotten to him again, and there he was, in the store. Again the owner was nowhere to be seen, so the little guy carefully, cautiously removed the top of the barrel and again ran his finger through the molasses. Just as he was putting it in his mouth, my boss mysteriously reappeared. This time he said nothing as he picked the little guy up and dropped him right into that big barrel of molasses. As he was sinking out of sight, you could hear him praying, "Oh, Lord, please give me the tongue to equal this opportunity!"

Your Challenge

As I put my thoughts on Top Performance on paper, it has been my prayer and my plan to share some information and inspiration that will make a difference in your life. The need for both information and inspiration in our personal and corporate worlds is enormous. The opportunity to benefit many people is great. My prayer is that some idea has struck a responsive chord in you that will enable you to enjoy your life more and be even more effective today than you were yesterday.

Theodore F. MacManus wrote the following piece, "The Penalty of Leadership," as an advertisement, and though it appeared in the *Saturday Evening Post* on January 2, 1915, the message is timeless.

The Penalty of Leadership

In every field of human endeavor, he that is first must perpetually live in the white light of publicity.

Whether the leadership be vested in a man or in a manufactured product, emulation and envy are ever at work. In art, in literature, in music, in industry, the reward and the punishment are always the same. The reward is widespread recognition; the punishment, fierce denial and detraction.

When a man's work becomes a standard for the whole world, it also becomes a target for the shafts of the envious few. If his work be merely mediocre, he will be left severely alone—if he achieves a masterpiece, it will set a million tongues a-wagging. Jealousy does not protrude its forked tongue at the artist who produces a commonplace painting.

Whatsoever you write, or paint, or play, or sing, or build, no one will strive to surpass, or to slander you, unless your work be stamped with the seal of genius. Long, long after a great work or a good work has been done, those who are disappointed or envious continue to cry out that it cannot be done. Spiteful little voices in the domain of art were raised against our own Whistler as a mountebank, long after the big world had acclaimed him its greatest artistic genius. Multitudes flocked to Bayreuth to worship at the musical shrine of Wagner, while the little group of those whom he had dethroned and displaced argued angrily that he was no musician at all. The little world continued to protest that Fulton could never build a steamboat, while the big world flocked to the riverbanks to see his boat steam by.

The leader is assailed because he is a leader, and the effort to equal him is merely added proof of that leadership. Failing to equal or to excel, the follower seeks to depreciate and to destroy—but only confirms once more the superiority of that which he strives to supplant.

There is nothing new in this. It is as old as the world and as old as the human passions—envy, fear, greed, ambition, and the desire to surpass. And it all avails nothing. If the leader truly leads, he remains—the leader. Master-poet, master-painter, master-workman, each in his turn is assailed, and each holds his laurels through the ages. That which is good or great makes itself known, no matter how loud the clamor of denial. That which deserves to live—lives.

Yes, leadership has its penalties, but fortunately, it also has its rewards. Here's hoping—and believing—that the principles taught in *Top Performance* will help you reap those rewards.

ACKNOWLEDGMENTS

In many ways this is the most unusual and exciting book I have written. Unusual because for the first time I worked with a coauthor and, in this update, with two men whom I love and respect. Without the contribution and assistance of Jim Savage, this book would not have been written. And now, with the unique talent of Bryan Flanagan and Krish Dhanam, the content is greatly enriched. My gratitude for each of them is significant.

As always, Laurie Magers, my ever-faithful, always dependable administrative assistant, did a magnificent job. When called upon, Kay Lynn Westervelt, who worked closely with Laurie, also did a beautiful job, as did Julie Norman, my editor and daughter. I owe a particularly heavy debt of gratitude to my friend and mentor Fred Smith, whom I hold in high regard, for his willingness to contribute thoughts and ideas throughout the book. A very special thank-you to Leo Presley, president of the consulting firm Presley & Associates, who encouraged us and gave important direction on getting involved on a larger scale in corporate America. Leo is one of the brightest men I know.

I am also grateful to Ron Ezinga, the past president of the Zig Ziglar Corporation, whose steady hand at the helm and encouraging guidance while we wrote this book kept us at least partially on course in meeting our guidelines. Then, of course, there's my wife, Jean, "the Redhead," whose willingness to tolerate some intolerable demands on our time together, combined with her loving support, not only made the book possible but also made it an exciting experience. To the other members of our staff and to the numerous authors who contributed through your articles, thank you.

NOTES

Chapter 4 Look for the Good

1. The I CAN course is currently distributed by an independent organization, The Alexander Resource Group, headed by Bob Alexander. For information on the course, go to www.yesican.net, or contact Bob Alexander, President, The Alexander Group, 4566 Oxford Circle, Macon, GA 31210, phone: 478-737-9081.

Chapter 7 On Great Leadership

1. To learn more about the DISC Model of Human Behavior, go to ZiglarTraining.com /disc.

Chapter 9 The Five *P*'s of a Top Performing Business

1. Download your own Wheel of Life here for free at www.Ziglar.com/ChooseToWin .com.
2. Jim Collins, *Good to Great: Why Some Companies Make the Leap . . . and Others Don't* (New York: HarperCollins, 2001).
3. Get a free Purpose Statement Worksheet at Ziglar.com.
4. Find out Zig Ziglar's seven-step criteria for choosing the right coach at Ziglar .com.
5. Download a free Guide to Building a Top Performance Culture at www.ZiglarTraining .com/smallbusiness.
6. Download a free Business Planning Worksheet at www.ZiglarTraining.com/smallbusiness.
7. Get a free Business Systems Assessment and Checklist at www.ZiglarTraining.com /smallbusiness. This assessment reveals fifty important systems that are required for a phenomenally successful business.

Chapter 11 Recognizing, Rewarding, and Role Modeling for Top Performance

1. Printed by permission from Dr. Michael H. Mescon, dean, College of Business Administration, Georgia State University, and Holder, Ramsey chair of private enterprise, and

Dr. Timothy S. Mescon, assistant dean, School of Business Administration, University of Miami, and published by Mescon Group Inc., Atlanta, Georgia.

Chapter 12 Getting to Know You . . . and Me Too!

1. Ziglar Inc., 15400 Knoll Trail Drive, Suite 103, Dallas, TX 75248. Phone: 972-233-9191. Website: www.ZiglarTraining.com/smallbusiness. Facebook: www.facebook.com/ZigZiglar.

Chapter 19 The Secret to Management Motivation

1. Adapted from Assuring Customer Loyalty, Ziglar Inc., 2000.

Zig Ziglar was an internationally renowned speaker and author. His client list included thousands of businesses, Fortune 500 companies, US government agencies, churches, schools, and nonprofit associations. He wrote thirty-two books, including *See You at the Top*, *Raising Positive Kids in a Negative World*, *Secrets of Closing the Sale*, *Success for Dummies*, *Over the Top*, and *Zig: The Autobiography of Zig Ziglar*. Nine of his books have been on bestseller lists, and his books have been translated into more than thirty-eight languages and dialects.

Tom Ziglar is the proud son of Zig Ziglar and CEO of Ziglar Inc. He is an international keynote speaker, an executive coach, and the author of *Choose to Win*. Tom lives in Plano, Texas.

Howard Partridge is an international business coach who has owned his own businesses for over thirty-four years. He is the exclusive small business coach for Ziglar Inc. and the director of training operations at Ziglar. Howard lives in Houston, Texas, and Destin, Florida.

David Mattson is a bestselling author, sales and management thought leader, keynote speaker, and leader for sales training seminars around the world. As CEO and President of Sandler Training, he oversees the corporate direction and strategy for the company's global operations, including sales, marketing, consulting, alliances, and support.

Krish Dhanam, a native of India, was the vice president of Global Operations for Ziglar Inc. Today he is the CEO of SkyLife Success, president of Mala Ministries, and global adjunct with Ravi Zacharias International Ministries. He lives in Flower Mound, Texas.

Bryan Flanagan is a past director of corporate training at Ziglar Inc. Today he is the salesman and CEO of Flanagan Training Group. His clients find value in his ability to make training both educational and entertaining. Bryan lives in Plano, Texas.

Jim Savage has served as a teacher, coach, and administrator on the high school level. He was also special assignments coach for the NFL Washington Redskins football team under Coach George Allen. In 1981, Jim joined the Zig Ziglar Corporation, where he designed and delivered training programs. He currently resides in Houston, Texas, and is employed with Franklin-Covey.

FREE Tools and Resources

We hope you've enjoyed reading *Top Performance*!

 Take your performance even further with these FREE tools and resources that will help you

- Become a stronger leader
- Get your team engaged
- Increase sales
- Boost profits

Plus, you'll get **free gifts** that will inspire you, your family, and your team members.

Special Email Subscriber Offers

When you subscribe at **Ziglar.com**, you'll also get special offers on products and invitations to free training webcasts, and you'll be notified about upcoming Ziglar Training Events!

Ziglar Training Programs

 Ziglar Legacy Certification—Become an ambassador, trainer, or coach with Ziglar. You will be equipped to bring the life-changing message of Ziglar to your company or your community. Not only is ZLC a personal development mastery course but it also equips you to offer Ziglar Training and Coaching as a business.

 Choose to Win—The fastest way to success is replacing a bad habit with a good one. Let's face it, we all have habits that keep us from being a top performer. In Choose to Win, you'll go through each spoke on the Wheel of Life and choose better habits for each spoke: Spiritual, Mental, Physical, Family, Career, Financial, and Personal.

 Ziglar Small Business Training—The everyday demands of running a small business can be brutal. Learn the strategies, skills, and systems to build a predictable, profitable business that gives you more freedom in your life.

 Ziglar Corporate Training—To be a Top Performer, you must be able to communicate, sell, and lead effectively. Ziglar has partnered with Sandler Training to deliver the most powerful results-oriented training available today. Call 800-527-0306 or go to **Ziglar.com/Sandler** to learn more!

 **Visit Ziglar.com today for more information!**

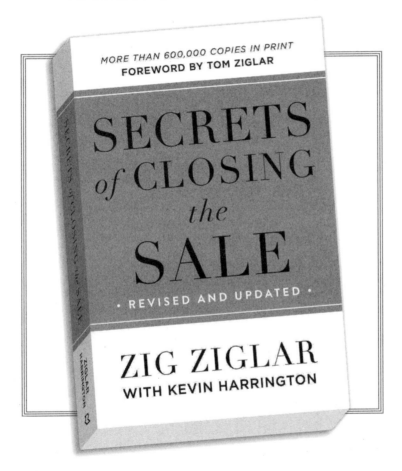